LEAN LIFE
Doing Life Better

Imagine we are driving down the road in the middle of the desert with no cell service, the radio is broken, and the air conditioner doesn't work. The windows are down, there is a dog between us, and we are letting it all hang out. We are both in awe of the simplicity of that moment and we're talking about life and what it's all about. This book is meant to be that discussion.

Most people's lives are so screwed up and they are living with a fraction of the joy they should know and experience. How could life be so marginal for so many when the very meaning of the word "life" echoes and resounds positivity? The answer is revealed on the cover picture of this book: we are not using our brains! This is really what this book is for me…a straight up, no BS shot at fixing the main reason life can gets so messed up. Make no mistake, I've made quite a few mistakes and I will admit them openly. The vast majority of the people that I hang with are pretty self-actualized and generally speaking they have their act together. None the less, there's plenty of unwanted junk messing up most of our lives. If we were to be honest with ourselves, we are the curators of dysfunction. I promise this will not be an intellectual exercise. No psychobabble. I don't understand it and it never helps me anyway. Rather, this is the perspective of an average guy who happens to be in love with Lean and fixing what bugs him. So if simple and practical is your preference, you're in luck! It is for me as well. If you have a modicum of curiosity and you want to see how to do life better, then *Lean Life* is the right book for you.

Tell the truth…
it will lead you to an amazing life

Save yourself a pile of money…
just be honest with yourself

The One Thing!

Often when I read books I'm not quite sure what the author's main point is, so I find myself racking my brain to figure out what they are trying to communicate. This can be frustrating and time-consuming. So when I write, I want my meaning to be as clear as possible. To make it easier for my readers I try to include a section that easily summarizes my thoughts into just one simple concept.

For example, in my first book, *2 Second Lean*, my goal was to teach the reader to "see waste and fix what bugs you." *(Go to the link at the end of the section to find 2 Second Lean.)*

In my second book, *Lean Health*, my goal was to teach the reader how to "treat your body like you would treat a Ferrari." *(Go to the link at the end of the section to find Lean Health.)*

In my third book, *Lean Travel*, my goal was to teach the reader how to "travel light and with a full heart." *(Go to the link at the end of the section to find Lean Travel.)*

Now, in *Lean Life*, I discovered that the missing piece for a fantastic life is to "know yourself." I believe we think we know what we want in life and the relationships that are important to us, but in fact, most of us are simply clueless. Having traveled to over 100 countries, I have witnessed vast numbers of dysfunctional lives, including my own. *(Go to the link at the end of the section to find Know Yourself video.)*

The question is why? Because we don't know our most important customer... ourselves. This concept is more profound and impactful than I would have ever imagined. It is crucial that we do this with precision and accuracy. There's no room for "kinda sorta." You have to know yourself with total clarity. It is the most essential work you do and will almost guarantee a life with deep meaning and happiness.

There is so much to discover in the pages ahead. It is a Lean revelation because Lean principles and ideas are at the core of solving so many problems. For example, my favorite Lean principle is "fix what bugs you." Basically, look at the things that bug you about your life and see what you can do to improve them.

Perhaps the greatest secret that most of us never really understand, is discovering that our problems should make us happy! Why? In the process of solving our problems we are given the opportunity to learn, exercising our brain, and improve.

My mentor and dear friend Mr. Amezawa, former VP of Lexus said: "People always ask me what the key to my success at Toyota was? My answer is: I always asked to be moved to where the worst problems were. I didn't avoid problems, I ran

Go to the problems... don't avoid them

to them. Other people called them problems, I called them opportunities to learn. Opportunities to have a significant life and improve the work for the thousands of people that I was responsible for."

As we finished our 26th Japan Study Mission, the team was about ready to get off the bus. Mr. Amezawa leaned over to me and said, "Paul san, you know this is the best team we've ever had." It was an amazing four days. Then, he gave a pithy life-changing thought to everyone on the bus: "Be happy when problems are in front of you. They are the opportunity for you to grow." What wisdom and insight! *(Go to the link at the end of the section to watch 2018 Year End Message video.)*

Be happy when problems are in front of you.

After a long flight home, I walked in the kitchen as my wife was making a coffee and she said, "Hey, the hot water dispenser is stuck and the water keeps running…" What immediately crossed my mind was, "There's no rest for the weary! I just traveled 14 hours and I can't even walk in the door and I'm already faced with fixing something." I thought "Man...I'll try to fix it, but I can see this costing about $200 to replace, not to mention cleaning out below the sink, getting on my back, loosening the screws, and disconnecting the plumbing...a very awkward and difficult job." Just as I was about to start cursing under my breath, I remembered Mr. Amezawa's words "Paul, be happy when you have problems!" In a split-second, everything changed. I put on a happy face and said, "What am I going to learn about hot water dispensers today?" For the next hour, I took it apart piece by piece and found the problem. I filed a small piece of plastic, sprayed a little lubricant, and it was back in working order.

Solving problems are simply an opportunity to develop yourself. One problem after another, small and insignificant, and the next thing you know you're a master. Taichi Ohno said it best, "You don't have to solve them 100%, you just need to improve and then build on every improvement for further improvement."

Mr. Miwa, calls it a "sparkle of discovery" where now the problem you were facing can be solved with new understanding.

One thing is for sure: if you're a Lean thinker, you don't ignore your problems, you fix them first! Even if they are relationship problems.

One of my good friends, at 82 said, "Paul, the problem with me is I married a nun and she never wants to have sex." Instead of dealing with the problem, he lived a lifetime of regret. Another friend and successful businessman, at 75, had everything you could imagine: a beautiful family, amazing business, and mobility. I remember asking him if he had any regrets in life. In a split second, he said, "I had a terrible sex life." I'm not purporting to have the answer for either of these men, but the point is, they both had problems and never dealt with them.

Mr. Miwa and "the sparkle of discovery"

They were both super smart people. When I'm speaking I often joke that Lean is not for super smart people, because most of them have "genius disease." They think they have all the answers instead of realizing they don't and that they need to be humble. As a Lean thinker, you cannot allow these problems to be swept under the carpet. Children hide their problems! We need to find solutions. Lean is so practical and often requires some really hard work, but as the solutions unfold they can make you smile when you see them working their magic. Whether it is on the shop floor of a manufacturing plant or with the ones you love, Lean ideas work!

In addition to summarizing the entire book with a phrase, I always put a simple, to-the-point summary at the end of every chapter called "The One Thing." It's a phrase or sentence that captures the meaning of the chapter and helps you remember and apply it in your life. So look for it at the end of each chapter.

Feel free to skip ahead and read "The One Thing" first before reading the rest of the chapter...whatever works best for you. The important thing is that you don't struggle to understand and you can easily apply the important stuff.

The One Thing
Problems are opportunities to learn.

paulakers.net/ll-one

Paul A. Akers

FastCap Press

Copyright © 2019 by FastCap Press
All rights reserved,
including the right of reproduction
in whole or in part in any form.

Paul Akers: Voxer or WhatsApp (+13609413748)
Emails will be deleted

Written by Paul Akers
First printing, May 2019
Manufactured in the United States of America

Lean Life comes in ALL flavors

You can read it or get even more insight by watching the videos and reviewing the resources on PaulAkers.net. Or listen to the expanded Audio-Book with extra "off-script" inspiration and added stories of innovation.

Check out PaulAkers.net for all the latest Lean Adventures

paulakers.net

ACKNOWLEDGMENTS

Editors

Leanne Akers, Lori Turley, & Filipe Marques

Graphics & Book Layout

Jayme Simpson

Illustrations

Paula Hansen

Special Thanks

In my first book, *2 Second Lean*, I was inundated by people asking the question, "how did you build a culture where everyone is engaged and improving on a daily basis?" So, I want to thank all the great Lean thinkers for their curiosity and desire to improve and learn who inspired me to write that book.

For my second book, *Lean Health*, my great friend and Brazilian beauty, Paloma, challenged me to make no excuses and start writing *Lean Health* immediately.

For my third book, *Lean Travel,* Sara Bailey (wife of the witty Brit, Ashley Bailey) said, "Paul, you need to write *Lean Travel*." Without giving me even a few seconds to digest this crazy thought, Ashley piped in, "No excuses buddy! You need to get *Lean Travel* written and published by your birthday, May 17th."

For *Lean Life*, my "thank you" goes to an unlikely individual that must go unnamed. Funny beyond belief, a friend that is as constant as gravity, with the honesty of a 4-year-old and insight about life that will make you laugh and cry at the same time. You know who you are, your secrets are safe with me. Thank you for setting this project in motion with that funny story about the relationship challenges that men and women are confronted with. I can never thank you enough for your deep honesty about life and for letting me be honest back to you. When I called you a "Lean pussy," you didn't get pissed at me, instead our relationship continued to get stronger, is unvarnished, and alive with deep respect. This book happened because of your honesty and because I was honest with myself. Thank you

Honestly, we are certifiably crazy

not only for your inspiration but also for all the other things you do and especially for your friendship!

Lastly, I am going to thank the most unlikely thing...honesty! Yes, honesty is imbued in both my friends and the most self-actualized people in the world. I seek it, I want it no matter how much it hurts because it is unequivocally the path to a meaningful life. I must caution the reader; in my honesty, I do so at the cost of looking a little foolish. I am willing to wound my pride in the eyes of some if what I write in the pages ahead helps just one person.

I have amazing friends and supporters all over the world and we all share a few things in common. We have a passion for improving the lives of people through the power of Lean thinking. Daily continuous improvement is my addiction and I know it's yours as well. I am very lucky to call all of you my friends and the relationships we share are the essences of life. Our goal is to "Do Life Better" and plant a great big smile on the face of every human being that has breath. Life and every aspect of it should be fantastic, interesting, enlightening, challenging, hopeful, inspiring and joyful. Yes, this is exactly how I feel about all the benefits I have gained along my Lean journey.

Friends at the YelloTools Lean Summit

To the Reader

If you read my first book *2 Second Lean*, the magic of it is that I made everything so simple:

FIX WHAT BUGS YOU
DAILY 3S'ING
DAILY MORNING MEETING
BEFORE & AFTER IMPROVEMENT VIDEOS

And you're done! There's nothing really too uncomfortable about any of those steps. If anything, it removes pain from your life because you're not struggling anymore with clunky processes or poor communication.

Lean Life is an entirely different animal and the difference is quite profound. The essence of the book can be boiled down to one simple concept: "Know yourself." The mechanics of doing it is quite easy. Take out a piece of paper and start writing about who you are. What is it about your current life that needs work and doesn't bring you joy? This is the "fix what bugs you" for *Lean Life*.

Getting yourself to do this is not easy and for most people, this could be an uncomfortable or painful process. You might be repelled by the notion of confronting the brutal facts about your life and the parts that are less than ideal.

People are not naturally going to jump to self-analysis like "fixing what bugs you," so readers beware! It's not as easy as *2 Second Lean*, but I guarantee, if you get it right, it's way more satisfying.

Most of the names in this book have been changed to protect the innocent and the guilty.

CONTENTS

	Doing Life Better	
	The One Thing	
	Acknowledgments	
Intro:	What is Lean?	1
Chapter 1:	Big Concepts About Lean Life	7
Chapter 2:	It's Your Brain!	10
Chapter 3:	Epiphany	13
Chapter 4:	Exercise This Muscle!	16
Chapter 5:	Weakness Oriented	21
Chapter 6:	The Super Power of Respect	25
Chapter 7:	The Life Factory	27
Chapter 8:	Clarity and Process	34
Chapter 9:	Go and Watch	38
Chapter 10:	Let's Have Fun	41
Chapter 11:	Are You Happy?	45
Chapter 12:	Give Me Shelter	57
Chapter 13:	Filling The Void	60
Chapter 14:	Paul's Conclusions	65

paulakers.net/ll-resources

WHAT'S THIS?

If you want to find any of my videos on any subject, just type in Paul Akers and search. For example: Paul Akers Lean Home

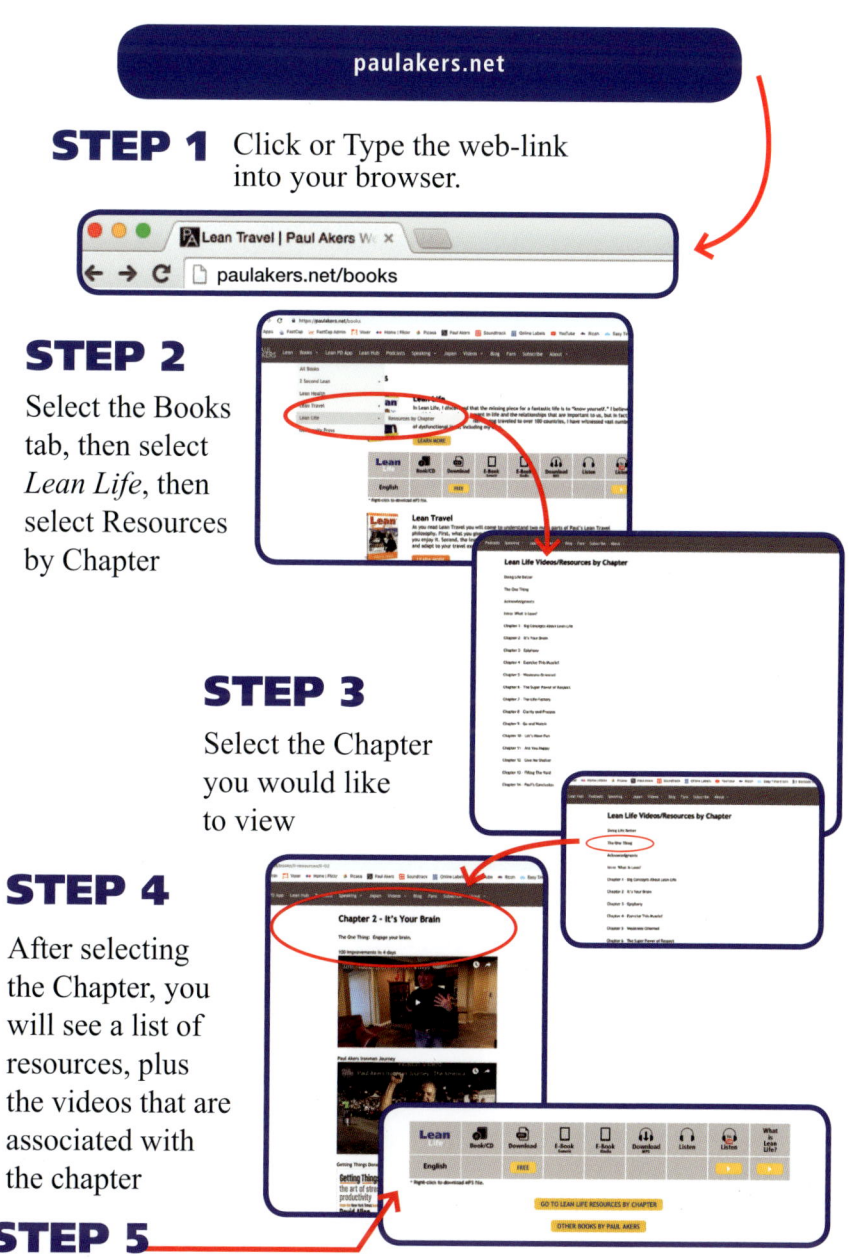

paulakers.net

STEP 1 Click or Type the web-link into your browser.

STEP 2

Select the Books tab, then select *Lean Life*, then select Resources by Chapter

STEP 3

Select the Chapter you would like to view

STEP 4

After selecting the Chapter, you will see a list of resources, plus the videos that are associated with the chapter

STEP 5

Under the books tab you can find all available electronic versions of Lean Life **FOR FREE!**

INTRO
What is Lean?

Perhaps the best way to answer this question is by contrasting a non-Lean thinker to a Lean thinker. A non-Lean thinker is someone who looks at any process and says, "It's good enough." They see problems and defects as inevitable and part of every process that can't be fixed. A Lean thinker is in pursuit of perfection. The methodology they use in this pursuit is continuous improvement. This single activity provides power for everyone who embraces it. They view relentlessly chipping away at your problems every day as the roadmap to utopia. *(Go to the link at the end of the section to watch What is Lean video.)*

In short, are you a "good enough person?" or a "continuous improvement person?" How you answer this question will determine the relevance of this book.

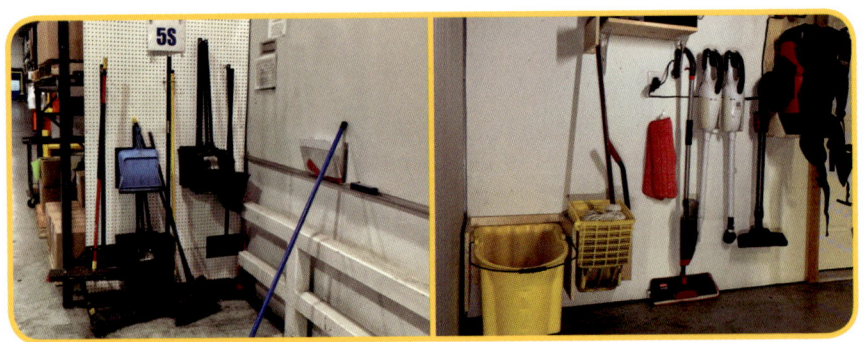

Struggling to get to the value   *Easy to get to the value*

The definition of Lean is doing more with less. If you are allotted one hour to do something, the Lean thinker will get twice as much done in half the time. Because continuous improvement is their passion the next time they will do it in a quarter of the time and improve the quality in the process. They do this by first identifying value-added and non-value added activity. Then they eliminate all the non-value added activity, which is referred to as waste. Lean thinking is a really simple concept...kindergarten simple. Think of it this way, there are red and green building blocks. Red blocks are waste and the green blocks are value.

Waste   Value

By eliminating waste out of every process, you reveal value-added activity, which is almost always a very small percentage of any process. Value-added activity is anything you do that changes or directly improves the product or desired outcome. For example, if you want to hang a picture, you walk into the garage to look for a screw gun, screws, a pencil, a tape measure, and a step ladder. All of that is non-value added activity because you haven't changed anything. The moment the screw starts to penetrate the drywall, that's value-added and that will take approximately one to two seconds. Most people would probably spend upwards of five minutes getting the tools. All this effort to deliver one to two seconds of value-added activity...hanging the picture. In addition, you would spend another three to five minutes cleaning up and putting everything away. Of course, if you don't clean up, then you are just going to create even more non-value added activity for future projects as you search for your misplaced tools. Yes, you may irritate the hell out of your spouse because your stuff is everywhere! Being generous, you could probably hang a picture in about eight minutes. More likely, 30 minutes, and I am sure at least one or two arguments would ensue along the way.

The vast majority of the activities most of us perform every day are non-value added activities, plain and simple. Could you imagine your garage having a nice little tool tote with screws, glue, a hammer, screwdrivers, and other essential tools neatly arranged? All you have to do is walk into the garage, grab the tool tote, walk to the room, drive the screws, and return the tool tote to its place in the garage. All of this takes only a minute or two...this is a Lean process. If you're a Lean thinker you're a long-term thinker. You're not thinking about the inconvenience of creating the tool tote, you're thinking about the benefits that the tool tote will give you over the course of your lifetime.

Basically, we spend a lot of time in life spinning our wheels. Whether it be answering emails, cleaning the bathroom, making a doctors appointment, preparing a meal or, most importantly, building and supporting the relationships with the people we love, most of our time is actually spent on non-value added activities. Why is so much time wasted? The secret is you must slow down to go fast. For 99% of people on this planet, this is totally counterintuitive. At my company, FastCap, we spend the first hour of everyday cleaning, making improvements, and meeting as a team before we begin work. We haven't missed this for over 12 years. Essentially we are slowing down and preparing to work effectively. In the game of life we should be executing a clear plan and a thoughtful strategy. The second something is not working we need to slow down, stop, and ask why. *(Go to the link at the end of the section to watch FastCap's Morning Meeting video.)*

Teaching and training people at the morning meeting at FastCap

One of the most notable features of the Toyota Production System and Lean Manufacturing is something called the andon cord. It is a simple rope that hangs above all team members assembling cars. If

Pull the andon cord to slow down and solve the problem

the team member senses any problems, big or small, they pull the rope and it stops the entire assembly line. At this time a light flashes and the team lead comes running to assist the team member. The philosophy behind this practice is, it is better to stop the line and not produce defects then continue on and not deal with the problems. It is a problem first mentality. If you deal with problems now, you eliminate tremendous amounts of non-value added activities and it's more than likely you won't have to deal with them multiple times in the future. You become a future thinker instead of a present thinker. This is the essence of this book. Slow down, make a very careful evaluation of who you are and where you're going, and the rest will take care of itself.

Lean thinking seeks to eliminate the waste most of us tolerate or create. In the realm of everyday life and relationships, for many of us, it is time to pull the andon! This book charts times I pulled the andon and what I learned when I slowed down enough to fix my problems.

We make one mistake after another without reflecting on the time or resources we have wasted. At age 58, I have become alarmingly aware of the passage of time. As a Lean thinker, the idea of having a deep respect for resources is of paramount importance.

If you really want to see non-value added activity, just think about a trip to see the doctor. Most of everything involved is waste. In most cases, the doctor looks at you for about five minutes, makes a determination as to what the problem is, and prescribes treatment. Calling to make the appointment, filling out the paperwork for the hundredth time, sitting in the waiting room, walking into the examination office, waiting for the doctor to arrive, having the examination, checking out, paying, and then driving home is all just waste. The value-added activity for being seen by the doctor is to determine what is wrong with you. That takes the doctor about five minutes.

Here is a quick and very humorous example. Just recently, I got a comprehensive physical and the doctor was reviewing all the blood work and results line by line. When we got to my prostate score the doctor showed me the results. I asked the doctor what I needed to do to lower that or get a more favorable score. Without even a moment's hesitation, he looked at me, flashed a grin

"Use it!"

from ear to ear and said, "use it!" No, I'm not going to tell you what my score is...

-3-

A quick review of the
8 WASTES

The 8 wastes can generally be found in most of everything we do. They are robbing you of valuable time on this earth. Worse yet, they almost always add complexity while simultaneously sucking the joy right out of you. You might as well jump on the proverbial hamster wheel because you are spinning round and round and getting nowhere.

If you really want to be remarkable in everything you do, consider applying Lean to your daily life. The thoughtful individual that becomes keenly aware of these wastes, and can spot them at the drop of a hat, has the greatest shot at having a very effective and satisfying life. Here is an exaggerated example of the 8 wastes in relationships as explained to me by my good friend LJ.

8 wastes of relationships according to LJ

1. OVERPRODUCTION:
I piss my wife off because I'm not really listening very closely and this overproduces a bunch of negative emotions.

2. TRANSPORTATION:
She transports those emotions to every room of the house and it doesn't matter where I go she even finds me in the garage to tell me what a bum I am.

3. INVENTORY:
She holds them in inventory for the next week and a half. It's a real pain in the ass.

4. DEFECTS:
I try to console her and explain to her why I screwed up so badly, but that only makes it worse and now I'm a double asshole.

5. OVER PROCESSING:
I jump in the car and try to figure out where I could possibly buy something: flowers, candy, chocolate, or candles...anything to get me out of the doghouse.

6. MOTION:
I suck at wrapping gifts and it takes me four times longer to wrap a gift that my wife would do in 30 seconds.

7. WAITING:
My woodworking project has now been on hold for over three days while I try to fix my screw-up.

8. UNUSED HUMAN POTENTIAL:
My wife has always been convinced of my unused potential, but now I'm even convinced of it...nothing but red blocks!

So in case you were wondering how The 8 wastes might possibly apply to your home life and your relationships, I hope it is now abundantly clear. *(Go to the link at the end of the section to watch How to NOT memorize the 8 wastes video.)*

There are three more concepts we must understand:

MURI
Muri is the Japanese word for burden or to be heavily weighted down. This is often seen in a relationship when we buy too much stuff and create financial stress. In addition, we then have too many things that require our attention to manage. It is important to note that we created this burden ourselves and invited Muri to come home and live with us.

MURA
Mura is the Japanese word for unevenness. When things go up and down, it can manifest itself in emotional tension, which produces the 8 wastes. An example would be when someone doesn't pick up their socks or underwear, causing their spouse to go into orbit (and that's not a heavenly orbit). The value-added activity was the four seconds it would have taken to pick up after themselves. The thinking person would remain in the lover role and not be thrusting their spouse, back and forth, between the roles of lover and maid...lots of unevenness and lots of waste. The lack of respect produced an afternoon of tension and attitude.

MUDA
Muda is the Japanese word for waste. If you have burdens and unevenness in your relationship you are going to have mountains of waste. Instead of having a relationship filled with joy and tenderness, you might as well be the producer, director, and actor of a daily shit show.

I am amazed at the application of Lean to the typical relationship. It's almost hard to believe the parallels.

Personally, I find this very interesting because I am lucky enough to have experienced financial success, and could have anything I desire. Because of this I

accumulated a lot of things. Unknowingly, all this inventory and overproduction created burden because I had to manage it and it distracted me from the things that were really important, like my relationship with my wife. Muri moved in. I've then further complicated my life by shifting a lot of this responsibility to my wife, so now she is burdened by Muri. Now we both share in the burden of making sure the cars, plane, motorcycle, and houses are being paid, and on and on...combined with running a growing business, that doesn't leave much time to relax and have a latte at a coffee stand together. This aggravated both of us because we were tired and out of time.

Now that we have all these unwanted guest living in our house, let's get started with *Lean Life*!

The One Thing
You have some unwanted house guests!

paulakers.net/ll-Intro

CHAPTER 1
Big Concepts About Lean Life

At the outset, there are a few things you should know about this book.

The Problem

Most people squander life. In the Lean language, most of the potential of our lives is never realized and simply wasted.

The Solution

Know yourself and experience the holy triad.

These two ideas are the main points in this book. Never fear, you will learn all about how to know yourself and the holy triad in short order. I promise these two ideas will be easy to understand, but very few will actually apply them because it will require you to fundamentally change the way you live and think.

It is not enough to just think Lean thoughts, you must convert hundreds of Lean thoughts into tangible actions that will teach you what does and doesn't work.

In the writing of this book, I'm working on three distinct improvements in my life. First, my posture. Standing up straight and not slumping. Mr. Amezawa and I were walking down the street and he said, "Paul, posture!" I immediately began to work on improving my stance. I also took before and after photographs of myself to see how badly I was hunched over. Now, when I walk, I am repeating to myself the word "posture" with Mr. Amezawa's distinct Japanese accent ringing in my head.

Second, eating more slowly. I am transitioning to eating with chopsticks and I take at least 30-40 minutes for every meal. The target is to enjoy my food more and its works fantastic.

Third, shaving more precisely and not leaving little straggling hairs around. It's working great. I am always looking with the magnifying mirror for hairs around my nose. In addition, I've switched to using coconut oil for shaving cream. It works much better and gives me a smoother and more comfortable shave.

I wrote this book to coalesce my ideas into one place about what I have learned about from my Lean life experiments, wishing I had this information in my early twenties. Wow, would my life be different today!

My life is great, but I do regret the time wasted because I didn't understand the simple and profound concept of Muda. I thought Muda was just part of life, instead of something that required my keen attention to eliminate waste and derive the maximum yield from everything I did. I could have done so much more with a fraction of the time, effort, struggle, and money.

Honestly, I have what most people regard as the important stuff down cold: a good education, hard work, and great investments. I read like a crazy man, I counsel with wise people, and I am intensely focused. I did all the right stuff. But if I equate my life's journey to driving a Ferrari, I had the potential of going 200+ mph. While I wasn't going the speed limit during the first 40 years of my life, I was doing more like 65 mph, nice and steady, making good progress. At 40 years old, I started learning the power of Lean thinking and overnight I doubled my cruising speed to 130 mph. Then, at 46, at the end of my power years, I started asking, "what if?" and I discovered this Ferrari could do 110 mph in the corners and 180 mph with ease in the straights. I now understand that I was not even close to discovering the full potential of my life. To be blunt, I was like a beginner pilot in command of the space shuttle. Through a little bit of navel-gazing and a whole lot of deep reflection (or "Hansei"), I unlocked a few secrets to life. This book is my high-performance driving course on how to do life better!

Would you drive a Ferrari in the slow lane?

What motivates me is the belief that life is short and to waste a single second of it is a tragedy. It's show time! Just today I heard another story from a friend of mine. The wife loves to travel but the husband hates to travel. They're both 80 years old and the wife now has deep regrets because her dream of traveling the world was never fulfilled. Why? Because she never understood the power of problem-solving through the eyes of a Lean thinker. I beg you to go live your life with no regrets, solve your problems...there is a way.

I believe that most people find happiness when they feel their life is improving. Conversely, people are filled with unhappiness when their life is stagnating. I have yet to find a single example in my life where this is not the case. So wouldn't it make sense to apply continuous improvement or Lean thinking to every aspect of your life? This is a very simple statement, but worthy of your close consideration.

Productivity = Sense of Wellbeing
Hyper Productivity = Profound Satisfaction
Serious Personal Improvement = Crazy Happiness

I believe that Lean thinking is natural for about 2% of the population. That 2% is never satisfied, intensely curious, and have are strongly prone to action. These people also have two other distinct characteristics. First, when their eyes are opened to see their weakness, they get really pissed and focus their efforts on relentlessly improving their shortcomings. Focusing on your strengths is a popular fallacy but it's the weakness mindset that delivers extraordinary results. If you fit this description, then you will probably enjoy my musings in *Lean Life*.

So what is a Lean life? When you realize you are the master of your own circumstances and stop with the BS excuses and get really honest. Take the limited resource known as life and apply a lot of deep thinking to it. Add in deliberateness, a few power processes, total resolve and create an extraordinary life.

> ### The One Thing
> Life is short and to waste a single second of it is a tragedy.

paulakers.net/ll-01

CHAPTER 2
It's Your Brain!

I can't teach you anything, I can only show you what I'm doing. What you do with the information is entirely up to you. The moment I become the teacher, I am elevated above you. My desire is to simply be an example, not a teacher. This is less pressure for me and probably more appealing to you.

Lean Life lays out how I brought a lot more happiness to my imperfect life. My life is improving in all the important areas: career, health and my relationships (holy triad). Most people's lives are in a slow steady decline in at least two of these areas. They have a list of things that they wish they could change. I personally don't feel that way. Why? Because I started using my brain and stopped allowing my emotions to take over my daily decisions. To quote Edwards Deming, I gained "Profound Knowledge" about the workings of life.

W. Edward Deming
"Profound Knowledge"

In my observation, most people make 60% of their decisions based on emotions and only 40% based on deep thinking. I can hear many of you saying, "Paul, I think deeply about life" and my retort is, "show me the evidence!" We tend to be whimsical creatures that are easily pulled and persuaded by the tugging of our hearts. I have concluded that if we could flip that ratio to 60% intellect and 40% emotion, we would all have a lot better life.

Here is an example I can give that everyone can relate to. You have personal problems with a co-worker but instead of dealing with it straight up you keep putting it off. The very act of putting it off creates wasted time and emotional energy, not to mention a lack of focus on your work and your obligations to create value for your customers. The fact that you're not willing to deal with this directly is the 60% emotional side...your emotions are in the driver's seat. You're certainly not thinking long-term about the issue and you're definitely not using your brain. If you don't deal with it now it's just going to get worse and you know it! If your brain was in the driver's seat, you would deal with the co-worker.

I can hear you saying, "but Paul, it's hard." To that I would say, "struggling throughout life and being perpetually frustrated is much harder!" For the record, I am one of the most passionate people you could meet. I infuse passion and emotion into everything I endeavor. However, I don't allow my emotions to make the decisions.

There is one quote that my good friend and mentor Norman Bodek shared with me that encapsulates this whole idea of taking control of your brain to the benefit of your life, "The mind is a terrible master but a wonderful servant." Translated, if you don't take control of your mind, it will run wild with all kinds of crazy urges, like eating a half gallon of ice-cream while standing in front of the fridge. It is up to each of us to harness our brain so it effectively serves us.

Norman Bodek

Lean supports freedom and intense creativity

I can hear the critics, "Paul, you are a machine, you are too structured, do you ever chill and take a break? When everything is always so structured, where does spontaneity and creativity fit?" The answer is everywhere and with everything.

It's all these processes that support my amazing life and allow me to have total freedom. I don't struggle with all the common things that most people struggle with. I'm not running around with my hair on fire and my life doesn't resemble a soap opera. My business runs smoothly, my employees are extremely well trained, my house is immaculate, my closets are clean, and my tools are in order. When I go to wash my car, there's an entire car washing station that has been set up so I'm never looking for anything and it's a total joy. This car washing station has been part of a continuous improvement project for over eight years. I have literally made hundreds of improvements to it...It just keeps getting better. *(Go to the link at the end of the section to watch 100 Improvements in 4 days video.)*

Paul & Leanne's dining and living room

Stop the struggle

I have the freedom to "blow with the wind" to any place, at any time! My thoughtfulness about all of life's details allows me not to be bogged down in all the mundane routines of life. Just last year I visited 30

Paul's first Ironman Triathlon

countries and did two Ironman Triathlons and countless other adventures. *(Go to the link at the end of the section to watch Paul Akers Ironman Journey video.)*

Recently, in an interview I did with David Allen, author of *Getting Things Done*, he made a profound comment that I'll never forget, "You can't make a mess in a mess." When things are in total order, you have total freedom. *(Go to the link at the end of the section to find David Allen's Getting Things Done.)*

Paul's interview with David Allen, author of "Getting Things Done"

As I continue to constantly improve all my processes, I gain the freedom to be hyper-creative. I learn to be thoughtful about all the small things...So let's get on with doing life better!

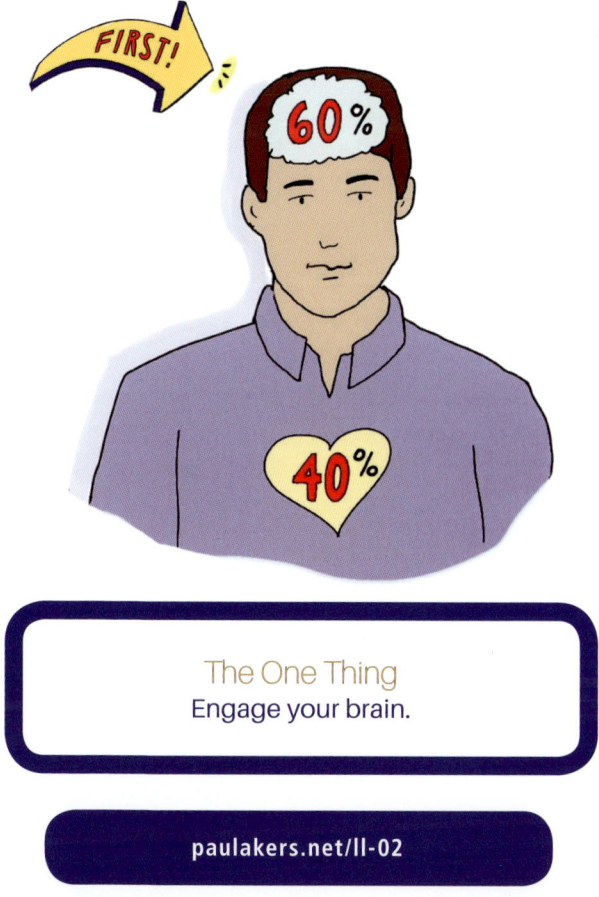

The One Thing
Engage your brain.

paulakers.net/ll-02

CHAPTER 3
Epiphany

Twice in my life, I've had an epiphany: an experience of sudden and striking realization.

The first one was when I was 37 years old. I was driving down the road and I heard a non-audible voice say, "I don't make junk...I made you with a purpose to do something great." At that time, I was questioning what direction I would take to create a strong lasting future? Would I continue to be self-employed or try to go to work for a local oil refinery and provide a more stable future for my family.

Those words were so reassuring. The irony was that I had applied for a job at a local refinery which would give my family great stability. This was a highly sought after job where over 800 people applied. I was one of two people that got an interview. I was well-qualified and knew many people at the refinery were pulling for me. I thought it would be next to impossible for me not to get it. Shockingly, I was not chosen and I had to readjust my sights on what the future would hold. I suppose this epiphany could not have come at a more perfect time.

I still hear those words today as if they were just spoken. I will never forget them. If they were written in the sky or tattooed on my hand, they could not have been more clear, "I don't make junk...I made you with a purpose to do something great." I wish I could explain it, but I can't. I can only tell you that they were more clear than anything I ever heard in my life. From that point forward, I stopped questioning my ability and my capacity to do something great. I never again listened to the naysayers and the people who said I was stupid or my ideas were not good. I saw every situation as an opportunity to improve the way I did my work and the way I conducted my life. Everything changed at that moment.

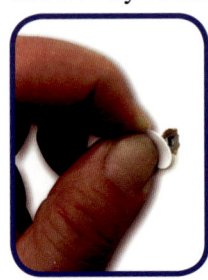
Paul's first invention the FastCap

A few months later, I invented my first successful product–the Fastcap–a peel and stick cover cap to cover screw holes inside cabinets. If I told you the number of people that thought I was crazy to quit my existing job as a cabinet maker to pursue this, I could fill a small auditorium. But having had my epiphany, I was done living in fear. Twenty years later, as I write these words, FastCap does tens of millions of dollars with 800 products and distribution in 40 countries. Needless to say, that was one amazing epiphany! *(Go to the link at the end of the section to watch History of FastCap video.)*

A short while ago, I had my second epiphany. In the scheme of my life, this one is equally as important because it unlocked my ability to understand life. As I observed many of my peers, people who are notable with their business success, I saw a pattern. No different than the famed scientist, Alan Turing, who broke the enigma code during World War II, I felt like I broke the code to understand life, in a much simpler format than Turing, but equally as important in my little world.

Most people with reasonable ambition have built a successful business or career. However, the vast majority of them did it by neglecting their health and relationships. They could be categorized into one of the following:

CAREER	HEALTH	RELATIONSHIP
Successful Career	Overweight	Unhappy.
	Sick	Miserable.
	Unhealthy	Frustrated.
	Obese	Defeated.

Feel free to mix and match the last two categories any way you want.

It is was rare to see a person at the peak of their career and who was also fit with remarkable health. It is even more unusual for them to have remarkable relationships.

Remember, I'm not talking about good, I'm talking about great. In his landmark book, *Good to Great*, Jim Collins makes an interesting observation which I will paraphrase, "The difference between good and great is massive, but it does not require a significant increase in effort or time. It does require a deep understanding of how things work and that requires deep thinking." *(Go to the link at the end of the section to find Jim Collins' Good to Great.)*

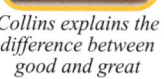
Collins explains the difference between good and great

It is not as though you have to expend 50% more energy to attain great health and have great relationships, but you do need to spend 50% more time to gain a deep understanding, some upfront planning, and developing a system to support excellence and eradicate mediocrity. The beautiful thing is when you invest this time, the payback is compounding because happiness begets more happiness. It's long-term thinking at its very best...the relentless pursuit of quality. A super high-quality life that is improving in the most important areas.

People focus too much on to-do's

Could this be the holy grail, the holy triad of excellence, the three legs of life? If individuals could find excellence in their career, health, and relationships, I see life's flywheel spinning with the least amount of effort. I have observed that most people let the superpower of this holy triad elude them their whole life. They spend more time on their to-do lists than on a deep understanding of their life plan. It was all beginning to make perfect sense. *(Go to the link at the end of the section to watch the Holy Triad video.)*

Why are so many people living with compromised health and dysfunctional relationships? The answer is the combination of the following 5 excuses:

1. We only have enough time to focus on one of these important areas.

2. We accept societies idea that declining health and relationships are par for the course.

3. We are masterful at covering up our deficiencies with baggy clothes, fake smiles, and small talk.

4. We are not predisposed to thinking deeply about the important issues in life, thus we lack profound knowledge about ourselves, so we can't improve our precious lives.

5. We have accepted the compromise that we can't have it all and, even if we could, it would be way too much effort and struggle.

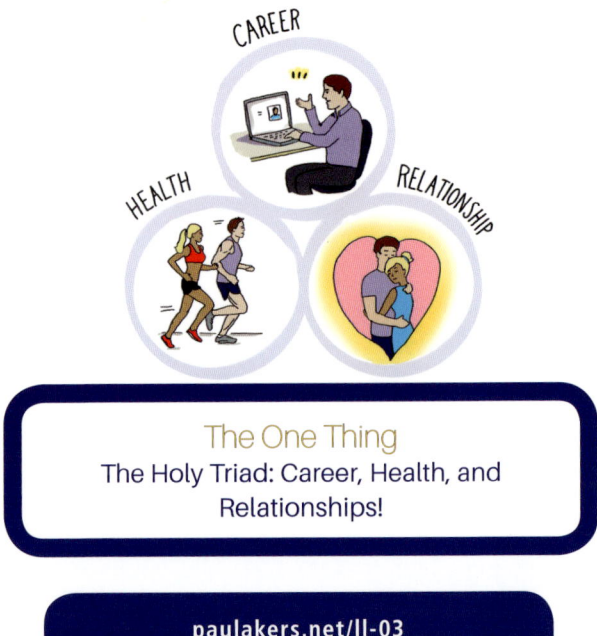

The One Thing
The Holy Triad: Career, Health, and Relationships!

paulakers.net/II-03

CHAPTER 4
Exercise This Muscle!

Our society does not put a high premium on educating ourselves on the processes that are imperative to have great health and relationships. In essence, our peers are ready to give us a mulligan, because most of us have dumbed down our expectations of life. Honestly, this low standard disgusted me regarding my own life, so I set out to do something about it.

The contrast is easy to see in Japan: A train left the station 20 seconds early and the train company issued a national apology for any inconvenience it might have caused its customers. Not a single customer complained, but they still felt the necessity to both apologize and make sure it never happened again. In the United States, you'd be lucky to get an apology if the train was 45 minutes late, let alone leaving early. We need to change our standards and expectations and superior outcomes will follow. *(Go to the link at the end of the section to watch Japan Shinkansen Train video.)*

If you're successful in your business, finances, or your career, it is more than likely you had some kind of a plan or a roadmap. Most people have spent a reasonable amount of time reading books and educating themselves at conferences and universities regarding their life's work. However, most of us have not applied the same amount of diligence to deeply understanding our health and relationships, let alone creating a plan and executing it. Our idea of researching viable solutions is thumbing through a tabloid while checking out of the grocery store...give me a break!

Focusing so much on the roadmap you leave something out

In this book I suggest one simple mantra, "Exercise This Muscle!" (as I point to my brain). If we were to use our brains, even for just a fraction of what we use it for on the other things in our lives, the outcome would be astounding. This is the premise of the book: how to develop a plan to fully understand ourselves first and then the people we are close to.

This book is not a scientific treatise on psychology. It is simply my musings about my life and observations as a well-traveled layman. At the age of 46, I started my deep thinking about my life and happiness. For the record, I've been married since 1983, which is amazing in today's day and age. On top of that, I started our amazing company with my wife and she has been working alongside me the entire time and now even my children work for us. We are one big happy family but not all the time. We have overcome many difficulties. I think the important thing is that we're still together and, even more incredible, that we all work together every day. I know many family members that can barely manage the obligatory Thanksgiving and Christmas, let alone function at a high level every day together...God bless nepotism! I subjected my family to a real pressure cooker and, honestly, I don't think it was all that beneficial. The fact that we survived it is truly amazing, but for me, that's not good enough. I want everything in my life to be excellent.

Paul and Leanne at the beginning of FastCap

Harry Akers, Paul's father

I remember listening to my father tell me that he never strayed from my mother and that he was quite proud of that, but inside I knew he was very frustrated like many men are. He would tell me, "Do you know what I could have accomplished if your mother would not have held me back?" To the women reading this book, don't hold your man back. Encourage him at every opportunity to reach his potential. He will love you deeply for it. But, even more importantly, take the time to know him at a deep level. Men, the same is true for you, but times two.

I think of Henry Ford's wife and her deep belief in her man and look what he accomplished. The same is true for Carl Benz, co-founder of Mercedes Benz. His wife believed in him when he gave up and she drove his new invention into town to show it to the masses. This story of the woman, not making a difference, but being the difference between a man's success and failure, is repeated millions of times in history and it is worth taking note of it.

Carl and Bertha Benz

Henry and Clara Ford

The flip side of a man's pursuit to conquer the world also requires the man to be present for their spouse and to know them deeply. That means regularly going to dinner with your spouse, where there's no cell phone and you're talking about something other than business. I know, for me, I can be very myopic once I lock onto something, everything else becomes secondary and this is not allowed in the context of a Lean life. This seemingly benign activity will fail you. It is opposed to one of the most important tenets of Lean which is a deep respect for people. You don't just wake up one morning and have this deep respect. You practice it day by day. You begin to see that the universe is organized around the principle of respect and it is in your best interest to embrace this magical concept.

Paul and Leanne enjoying dinner at El Calafate, Argentina

You're not being respectful when you're looking down at your cell phone and you're out to dinner with the one you love. That cell phone in your hand is like a glowing neon sign that says, "the person on this phone is more important than you." My daughter has taught me this, by taking my phone from me when we go to any coffee shop. This may seem like some cute game, but it is a powerful reality that every person must fully understand. The small act of being totally present when you are with the one you love is the gateway to a life of love and success.

When cell phones become the main focus of your life

If twenty years ago a scientist said, "I'm gonna be able to get everyone in the world to have a hunched posture, looking down," most people would've laughed. But stop and look around at the posture of most people in the world. Young and old, we are hunched over our phone looking down. We look like primate knuckle draggers, not human beings looking each other in the eyes.

This is why I love Lean concepts: they are simple, practical and effective. This small pragmatic process is the equivalent to delivering a dozen roses every time you're together. Life should be remarkable for both men and women and accepting anything less than excellence is the exact bubble I want to pop. Why do so many people settle for average when excellence is easily available? That is why I am writing this book because I struggle like many people. There is a better way. I'm convinced of it and I found it.

I have always had a strong predilection to improve everything in my life. I love it when things get better. I'm sure it is partly because chemicals are naturally released inside of us when we experience a move in a positive direction. Basically, I am a drug addict, but on the natural substance of satisfaction. My life is on a steady incline of accomplishments with my business, my health, and in most of my relationships...but not always. Basically, I stopped getting pissed and riddled with excuses and started thinking deeply about what I was really doing.

The people who will probably be most drawn to this book will be men who are unhappy with their current health and relationships and want to figure out how to make it better. They just want to know what the hell they did wrong when they were filled with such good intentions. These men will be typically in their 30's, 40's, and 50's. All the people who have read this book, prior to its release, were in this age demographic and the book resonated with them. These men would say to themselves, "I was hoping things would have turned out much better than they did." That is the problem. A great relationship requires much more than hope management and wishful thinking.

I would love the book to be relevant for women as well. Whether or not it will be, I'm not sure. I will do my best to integrate their thinking into the content because it's so important that men truly understand a woman's perspective. I've had many women pre-read the book and I've got very favorable comments. Here's one from Ashley.

Hey Paul!

I have to say I really enjoyed reading your stuff last night. It was so strong, but the best part is, it's so true! If something sucks or someone's lazy, you call it as it is.

I find your delivery to be intense, straight forward, and so honest. I think reading this will either light a fire under your butt or intimidate you because you're not sure if you have it in you to make these fundamental changes. I am a prime example. If I was reading this a few years ago, I would have felt that this was bigger and better than what I could achieve. Today, after one year of doing Lean in all aspects of my life, I have confidence and am able to relate much better. At the end of the day, your words are not for the average pedestrian, but for people who have begun their Lean journey and are ready to graduate to the big leagues.

Thanks,
Ashley

Ashley's comments have reaffirmed that women also appreciate straight talk and truth-telling. But men have conveniently branded them as irrational. This removes men from taking responsibility for the lousy outcomes. In the Lean world, we refer to all problems as management problems. Management has set up bad systems and processes and expects people to work well within them! In a relationship setting, more often than not, the man is leading and more dominant and, as a result, has more responsibility.

At the end of the day, this book is a work in process. I'm sure shortly after I publish it and people begin to read it, I will learn much more about how to have a great life in all aspects including our relationships. That's OK because I'm all about continuous improvement. It doesn't have to be perfect, our lives just need to be moving in the direction of improvement. Venu Srinivasan, a good friend and one of the top industrialists in India at TVS Motor, explained to me we build knowledge through experimentation. We never get it right the first time, the second time, or even the hundredth time. But if you keep trying, you will build knowledge so you can change your life.

Venu Srinivassan chairman of TVS Motor

The One Thing
Know yourself.

paulakers.net/ll-04

CHAPTER 5
Weakness Oriented

Mens weekend discussing problems

I was sitting around a campfire with a bunch of guys listening to them talk about their relationships with their spouses. To be honest, nothing I heard surprised me because, as I travel, I meet men and women who are unhappy about their relationships. A few report to be happy, but when you drill down, most of them have a point or two of misery but won't openly admit it.

Let me give you a humorous (or maybe not so humorous) story to illustrate my point. When I was in Sri Lanka, I was with a taxicab driver and we struck up a conversation about our families. I asked him how long he had been married and if he had any children. He said he had been very happily married for about 12 years. I asked him the key? He retorted back that he had two girlfriends: one in the city we were in and one in the city we were traveling too. I sat there slack-jawed...what the hell! He said, "My wife doesn't like to have sex and I can't take it, so I had to outsource it." Wow, talk about speechless! Honestly, that describes what I have found as I interview men around the world. Most will not say it out loud, but it is exactly how they feel. What I discovered is not complicated or difficult to understand, but it is revealing. If you think this book is going to be all about the fact that men are not getting it, you're wrong.

Taxi driver

I remember when I was on a family vacation in Mexico, about ten years ago. We all piled into a van and our driver's name was Angel. Before long we struck up a conversation with him and my wife asked, "Angel are you married?" He flipped down his visor and said "This is the picture of my wife. She's married but I'm not."

I made a discovery after observing and talking with hundreds of men and women in over 70 countries. Most people are deeply frustrated about something in their lives. These people cut across all religions and demographics. Money or religion appear to have very little impact on the facts. Believe me, I would love to report differently, but it's just not what I have experienced.

I would love to tell you that we Christians have it figured out more than everyone else, but the answer is, we don't. I can regale you with stories of family and friends, who are Christians, who are dysfunctional in their relationships.

It appears that an awful lot of us in the human race seem to be doing the wrong thing at a very fundamental level. That is the essence of this book. How we create a simplified process about doing life better, that the average person can deploy. Unfortunately, for many people, thinking deeply is just too much effort. It's easier to grab a bag of chips, sit on the couch, and watch a movie.

Most people have never looked deep into their soul and done a careful analysis of what it is that makes them happy and what they need. Probably because we are afraid of the answers and the action it will require us to take. It is just too uncomfortable. That change, more than likely, would first require a total about-face of our deeply ingrained habits and a hard assessment of our friends and family. I know this to be the case for myself, because it wasn't until I was 46 years old that I started to pen a document entitled, "Are you Happy?"

Stop spectating, live life

While I'm not a big proponent of value stream mapping, and we don't use that tool regularly at my company, this document is essentially my value stream map for myself. I took the time, for the first time in my life, to really analyze and get total clarity on what makes me happy. I discovered so many things about myself that I never knew.

Start good habits to further grow yourself

For example, I learned that one of my deep needs is to be respected intellectually by my peers. Reflecting back I would rehearse many situations where I felt inadequate in my knowledge and my ability to articulate ideas. If I wanted to overcome this frustration in my life it was necessary that I developed some different habits. Specifically, the counter-measure or habits that I changed were that I quit watching TV and I started reading a minimum of one book a week.

It was no more than five years after I developed these habits, that my speaking fee increased, and I consult with companies from around the world. Can you imagine if I had not taken the time to write this document that addressed my deficiencies and weaknesses? I also have become friends with extraordinary leaders from all over the world. My life would have been a vapid wasteland in comparison if I had not changed my behavior.

The result is I charted a new course to bring more happiness into my life and I was successful in doing so. Unfortunately, this little activity, that took me about three weeks, should have been something that I did when I was a young man.

I have shared this document with both men and women and it inevitably results in their deep reflection. Many would stare at me and say how did you get the courage to ask yourself such probing inquiries? It's simple, I realized two things: First, the alternative of doing nothing and reliving the same dissatisfaction day after day had zero appeal; Secondly, I understood that if I looked deep inside my psyche to answer these uncomfortable questions, it would give me the power and insight to bring lasting change.

The first question I asked was not what would make me happy, but rather what was it that made me unhappy, I focused on my weaknesses and deficiencies. The results I gained were total clarity on what makes me tick. Next, I laid out what I needed to do, on a daily basis, to correct those weaknesses.

I will lay it on the line, we don't understand our most important customer relationship. Well, it is true that our customer is our partner and we should position ourselves to serve them extremely well, but here is the hard thing to get your head around. *We* are our most important customer! To the extent we fully understand our needs and serve ourselves, that is the extent to which we can best serve our spouse.

I know this sounds self-serving, but I promise you that's not what I'm trying to say. Life is all about what you give, but you can't give what you don't have. If you don't have peace of mind, if you don't feel satisfied as a human being, and if you live part of your life in a vague haze of perpetual frustration, how in the world can you effectively serve the ones closest to you? A strong self, with a clarity of purpose and a clear process to achieve it, will allow you to give more abundantly to everyone around you. It doesn't matter what we do to serve our partner, we will always be frustrated if our needs are not being met at the most basic level.

Haze of frustration

I will share with you, in Chapter 11, a copy of the document "Are You Happy?" That I penned when I was 46 years old. I hope that everyone will take the time to write out a similar document. In doing so, you can gain clarity and build effective processes to dramatically improve your life and your relationships. If you can't wait, feel free to skip ahead.

It is essential that every human being takes a deep dive into their soul. My good friend, Ritsuo Shingo, once said, "You must know the facts and understand the facts." You need to get the facts, know them, and understand them very well. *(Go to the link at the end of the section to watch Ritsuo Shingo video.)*

Ritsuo Shingo

The One Thing
What makes you unhappy?

paulakers.net/ll-05

CHAPTER 6
The Super Power of Respect

As I interviewed men and discovered what it is that really makes us tick, I discovered that men often project a tough exterior when what they really long for and are often missing is a deep emotional connection. As I interviewed women and discovered what they really want I was equally surprised. My hope here is that women and men might gain a little more clarity on what it is that makes us tick.

Gaining totally clarity on what makes us tick

One of my most revealing answers came to me when I was interviewing a woman friend of mine named Jan. She is 70 years old and is very well put together. You can tell that when Jan was in her prime, she was pretty hot. I asked her what she wanted in a man and what is the most important thing a man can give her. I am somewhat familiar with women saying, I want them to treat me like a princess and have only eyes for me, but Jan's answers somewhat surprised me...she said respect.

I was surprised because this is a typical answer I would get from a man, but I had never heard that from a woman. The interesting thing is that her third husband, of about 5 years, also looked a little surprised at the answer. I asked her to explain. Jan said she first got married right out of high school and had 3 children. That marriage only lasted about 5 years. She then met a wealthy man who was at the top of the social ladder in the city where they lived. In the beginning, things were fine. Before long, Jan felt like none of her ideas mattered and she was little more than arm candy to her husband, who was 20 years her senior. After 5 years of marriage, they divorced and Jan was on her own, again as a single mom with 3 kids to raise.

Then Jan did what I think the answer is to all great relationships...she hit a Lean life grand slam. Jan went back to school, got an education, a great job, and earned the respect and admiration of her former husband. A few years later, they remarried and he never treated Jan disrespectfully again. Jan said they remarried and were happily married for 35 years until his death.

Lean Life grand slam!

Jan had total clarity on what was important to her. She identified and dealt with her weaknesses and played the game of life with knowledge and understanding.

When I first met her I found her very friendly and winsome. On a two-week trip with Jan and her husband, we got into a technical conversation and she said something that made me think she was not up to speed on the topic. For a moment, I started to be dismissive and I caught myself and reeled it back in. Two days later, I decided to interview her for this book and to get her opinion on life and relationships. When she gave me the "respect" answer, I was so thankful that I didn't say anything that she could interpret as a man looking down on her. Jan is a very capable woman and is deserving of all my respect. The trip we were on was a technical scuba diving trip. Most men would have shied away from this trip, but not Jan. She obtained her Nitrox Certification and was diving with sharks with all the other men. To say the least, Jan is a kickass woman and me looking down on her because she was not up to speed on one subject would have been gross negligence on my part. Now I know what's really important to Jan and that information is invaluable to us having a great relationship. *(Go to the link at the end of the section to watch Diving Socorro Islands video)*

Jan and the rest of the crew on a scuba diving adventure

The One Thing
Respect is a powerful concept. Learn it, live it, and fall in love with it's magical power.

paulakers.net/ll-06

CHAPTER 7
The Life Factory

I am a self-admitted linear thinker. Logic works for me and the thoughtful process of Lean thinking has served me well in my business, home, and personal life. At the same time, so you don't think I'm a machine, I'm also a musician, songwriter, and artist. I am very passionate and I approach everything with great enthusiasm. It really never occurred to me that a manufacturing process could be applied to my life, let alone my relationships. So here goes one of my boldest experiments.

We are all on the shop floor building our lives. We have been producing many

Paul playing his guitar off the coast of Antarctica

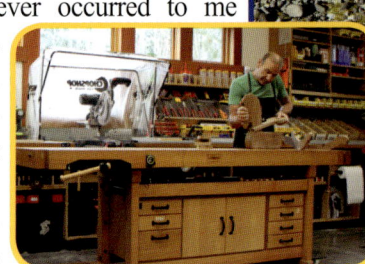

Paul working on a project in his shop

elements, from our health to our relationships. Some of us have been producing mountains of defects, resembling a car that is running on five cylinders when it is a 454 V8. The muffler has been tied up with baling wire and three out of the four tires are flat. Just like the car I described, our relationships run, but they certainly are not the first car most we would choose to go across town, let alone a cross country trip. Our life cars need some serious work. We have been poorly trained and have been thrown onto the manufacturing line: "Hey, here's some parts, now go figure it out."

Unlike this car, put some serious work into your life.

This is akin to putting someone with a beginners drivers license into a Ferrari, on the starting line of a Formula One race. Needless to say, the outcome would be disastrous. *(Go to the link at the end of the section to watch Porsche Driving School video.)*

Another way of looking at it may be a little more comical. The way we choose our mates is sometimes ridiculous,

Formula One race car at the starting line

even ludicrous when you really stop and think about it: "Wow! This girl is cute! She's got a nice rack, nice legs, pretty smile, and she's friendly." Hey buddy, you better look under the hood. There's a lot more to it than that! If it turns out that the electrical system was made by the English, the drivetrain was made by the Italians, the loan department was managed by the Greeks, and the efficiency standards were designed by the Americans, hey, guess what, you got one hell of a problem on your hands if you're going to buy that car.

Guaranteed, there is a lot more to it than looks, pretty smile, and great humor. There are other things that are just as important. For starters, the first thing men should do is carefully evaluate her mother. Ladies take a close look at the father and particularly how the father relates to the mother. If either of you ignores these points, you do so at your own peril.

I interviewed Vivian, a 38-year-old woman from Taiwan who was married for only three years before she got a divorce. I asked her, "Why?" She replied, "I don't know, I just lost the spark." I spent hours trying to figure out what could cause this beautiful woman to leave her good-looking husband with a successful career. For all intents and purposes, they had it all going on: money, looks, careers, and travel. But, for whatever reason, it only lasted three years. I asked her what would make her happy and she said, "I'm not sure!" This is not some ditzy lady. She is a highly educated, bright, financial analyst that speaks four languages and predicted the 2008 stock market crash. How could a seemingly smart educated person not be able to answer this simple question? This really gets to the crux of the issue...we really don't know ourselves!

How do people lose the spark?

Being the persistent person I am, I continued to ask Vivian if at some point she could tell me what went wrong. Approximately a year later, she sent me a message detailing her thoughts and gave me permission to share them. I am so thankful and appreciate Vivian's honesty and candor. There is so much to learn from her answers. As you read them, imagine if she had this document before she got married and knew what was deeply important to her. What if her future husband read those words so there would be a deep understanding on his part as well? Imagine if her husband had also written a document outlining his innermost thoughts and shared it with her. I think there would have been a much higher likelihood of harmony, or a very early realization that the match was not as good as it needed to be.

Vivians's Answer
THE THINGS THAT MAKE ME HAPPY

1. Achieving something that I once thought was impossible.
2. Someone gives me his soul.
3. Achieving a goal.
4. Knowing someone will always be the pillar I can lean on.
5. Someone who respects all my wishes, even if they're silly, and does not judge me.
6. Feeling like I'm doing what I was born to do!
7. Seeing the good in people.
8. Meeting new people and chatting with them about their life and work experiences.
9. Negotiating and meeting a mutually beneficial agreement.
10. Going on an adventure.
11. Losing myself and focusing completely on something like learning a new foreign language.
12. Anything Egypt.
13. Anything caramel.
14. The sound of rain when I'm inside the house.
15. Taking a bath.

Vivian concluded by saying that the 5th one was by far the most important. I honestly believe that deep down inside we're all little boys and girls who want to run, play, and express ourselves. We want to take on a childlike curiosity, yet we need someone beside us who is not only willing to let us do that, but supports and encourages us to do it. I ask you how long did it really take Vivian

Vivian and Paul

to write this out? In a relatively short time, your life could be changed. This is exactly how I started my "Are you Happy?" document. These 15 points are really just a starting point. From here you can develop your list and all of a sudden the document becomes a clear process sheet for how to do life better. In the Lean world, what really happened was Vivian pulled the Andon cord. It's as if she said, "I'm done producing defects. I'm gonna find out what the real issues are and solve them now." You might even find that this will be the most therapeutic thing you ever do and it's a whole lot cheaper than going to a shrink, who's going to get you to blame everything on your parents.

I've been mentoring a guy for quite a while when he found a very nice girl and wanted to settle down. He counseled extensively with me and another friend. We gave him our best advice for hours on end. All he wanted to do was tell us about how great this girl was, but she was a little crazy, emotional up-and-down, and not very stable, but she had so many other positive attributes. I will never forget my friend's reply back to him, "Hey Bob, I married the same kind of girl and 30 years later I can't even negotiate a shower. I'm so freaking pissed off, I can't even begin to tell you." We warned Bob, over and over again, that this did not look good. Today, Bob calls me regularly to tell me, after only two years of marriage, all the problems they're having. I want to hang up on Bob or tell him, "you're wasting my time. I tried to warn you and you didn't listen to a word I said." Bob replies, "I know I screwed up big-time."

I interviewed Jim, a 75-years-old successful insurance salesman and I asked him what would make him happy? What does he want from a woman? He replied with total clarity. Peace! Jim was on his third marriage and finally figured out what was most important to him...harmony at home. I replied back to Jim, "What took you so long to figure this out?" He said, "I don't know, I just never thought about it until now."

News flash: Start thinking about it! You need to make sure you know what makes you happy and make sure you marry someone who is closely aligned with what you value. In the Lean world, we use the value stream mapping to map out value for the customer, but we never ask ourselves what is the real value for us! I have come to learn its significance and the importance of putting it down on paper.

Stories just go on and on. This one is probably the most outrageous of all. One time I was flying back first class from Mexico and I struck up a conversation with a 70-year-old man. He was the president of $1 billion consulting company, one of the most famous in the US. He also was on his third marriage. I asked him, "What is the one thing you want in a woman?" He said, "I want them to go with me." I asked him to explain and he replied, "With my first marriage, as my career started to take on a steep trajectory, I began to travel all over the world and my wife was not particularly interested in going with me. 1 + 1= 2. This is all very basic math. You get it! I then went on to repeat the same mistake with my second wife. I married a woman who did not want to go with me. Finally, on my third marriage, I found a woman who likes to travel and loves the excitement of going to new places and meeting lots of interesting people." The interesting thing about this guy, he is an expert on Lean. He never thought of applying basic value stream mapping to who he would select to be his life partner. Frankly, I can't pick on him too hard because I didn't either until I started writing this book. Remember what the subtitle of this book is, "Exercise This Muscle!" If you choose to ignore your brain and follow only your emotions, you will follow your emotions to misery.

Humor me for a moment. Our relationships are not some mystical happening, rather they are the result of the things we do and don't do. They are a product of our efforts or the lack thereof. Bad relationships are the result of poorly, ill-conceived processes set in place by ignorance. Or worse, by laziness and lack of effort or, in some cases, total stupidity. I think most people spend about the same amount of time working on a life process for developing a great relationship then they do ordering at In-N-Out Burger. Come on! This is the most important thing in our life. This is the person you will spend a lifetime with. It's deserving of serious rigor and diligence.

Focus on spending more time on any relationship

Having been around fast cars and raced them a fair amount, I know there are a few basic things you need to know and if you get those basics down you can do pretty well. Don't brake when you are cornering, smooth is fast, eyes up, and look beyond where you are driving. There is no difference in relationships.

There are a few basics men need to know and know well. I wrote this book not because I knew what those basic operating principles were, but because I wanted to discover them for my own relationships. I also found it incredibly fascinating that some of the very core principles of Lean manufacturing applied perfectly and directly to having great relationships: Respect, *Overproduction*, *Excess Inventory*, *Just-in-Time*, Kata routine, all these concepts are remarkably relevant to how we build a great life.

While the Toyota Production System is the greatest business management concept in the world, the concepts can apply in your personal life. Unfortunately, many men have ignored the respect component. It appears, by our actions, that many of us were thick headed about how to treat a woman with respect and build a great relationship. We dismissed females as highly

Complexity of women is similar to a 747

emotional, irrational partners who required genius level knowledge. We lacked the same highly trained attention and skill a 747 pilot knows about the complex knobs, buttons and computer screens in their aircraft. When we see the knobs, buttons, and computer screens we think, Oh sh*t, what's happening now?!

If your position from the outset is that you screwed up and you want to learn and improve, then maybe my words might be helpful. I haven't even finished writing this book and I've learned so much about myself and life, it is making my head spin. I just wish I had this insight when I was 18. Knowing what I know now would have saved me a lot of pain and suffering and, more importantly, I would have had a lot more joy and happiness.

How can we have a super happy and fulfilling life in all regards? The answer is, "know yourself!"

I find it interesting that when I teach people how to do Lean, the first thing they want to do is point out somebody else's waste. I always say to them, "forget about everyone else. You have enough waste of your own life for ten lifetimes." Your first priority is to know yourselves and develop processes that support our most important needs. What so many of us do is ignore the source of the problem, which is ourselves, and try to fix somebody else. Caution! This will never work. Fix your waste and your problems first!

CAUTION!
Fix your problems, not others

This is not intended to be a scientific approach, rather I'm just a regular guy asking some tough questions and getting some surprising answers. As in all my books, I try to identify the value and the non-value added activities. I also do my best to identify those things which are waste. One of the two pillars of Lean manufacturing is respect for people. If at any point you don't respect your partner, you are going to die a slow, painful death. Disrespect is the number one non-value added activity. If you get the respect component right, you're going to have a very good life.

I have a simple analogy for you to help you understand respect. In my second book, *Lean Health*, I said all you need to do is treat your body like a Ferrari. You would never put anything but the best fuel in a Ferrari. In *Lean Life*, we need to do the same thing. We need to treat our partner with deep and abiding respect. If I had a Ferrari, I would be very careful never to get into it with muddy boots or greasy hands. I would always make sure it was polished to perfection. If you think of your partner, the one you love dearly, in the same fashion, you would never say anything harsh or treat them flippantly...she is your Ferrari! You need to cherish her in the very same way. *(Go to the link at the end of the*

Paul before and after Lean Health

section to find Lean Health.)

A friend of mine, Thomas, read this chapter before it was published and felt that this particular point was helpful. He said, "You know Paul, I have a very good relationship with my wife Jenny, but I don't think I treat her like a Ferrari, maybe more like a Toyota Corolla. Jenny is very reliable, very dependable, but I think maybe I take her for granted and I don't have the specialness that you talk about when you referred to treating the one you love like a Ferrari." Honestly, Thomas'

Treat your partner with deep and abiding respect like you would a Ferrari

retort made me pause and realized I think I treat my wife like a Toyota Corolla too. I think I would have avoided a lot of pain and trouble if I would have had a deep and abiding, protective respect for my wife. Bottom line, our mates become familiar to us and we become a little flippant and careless.

My good friend Lina told me something that I've never been able to forget. She said, "Paul, never hurt a woman...they never fully heal." When I think of the words Lina spoke to me, I think of them in the context of taking a hammer to my beautiful Ferrari. I would never do that. But essentially isn't that what we do to our partners when we blow up or talk down to them? We say things we should never say. I am guilty of doing this, but I now have this paradigm shift that is helping me think more clearly about what I've done in the past and what I'm going to do from here on out. Treat the one you love like a prized Ferrari!

Thomas & Jenny

Paul & Lina

The One Thing
Are you treating your partner like a Ferrari?

paulakers.net/ll-07

CHAPTER 8
Clarity and Process

A few years back I received an email from my cousin, Pamela, in New York. She said, "You know what it is about you, Paul? You are crystal clear on everything." I found her comment to be extremely helpful because it verified exactly what I try to do. When I work with companies to help implement Lean, I am astounded at the lack of clarity in their communications and directives. Most people are happy coming back 3 or 4 times for clarification, instead of getting it right the first time. They will send 4 to 5 emails when they could just pick up the phone and get it right. This is a massive amount of wasted energy and time. I have no room for this in my life.

As you read this chapter, do so with this in mind. Also, remember nothing is couched in political correctness or intended to garner approval, rather it is an honest answer from the shop floor. I'm sure I will piss off tons of people. I am sorry that I can't please everybody, but I hope, as a result of my musings, to help some people, including myself.

As a result of many interviews, I discovered the real value that a man gives a woman and a woman gives a man. Let's face it, there is a reason we are together, and understanding it at a deeper level is infinitely important if one hopes to have a great life. What relationships are missing is clarity and process. Clarity on what's important and a process on how to make sure we can consistently deliver it.

I have discovered that keeping things simple allows people to grab a hold of the ideas and actually work with them on a daily basis. Simplicity attracts people; complexity repels them. My predilection towards simplicity is based on some very basic observations. How many people can remember the Apple logo? How many people can remember the Samsung logo? Apple has mastered simplicity in its retail stores and products. Taichi Ohno said, "Make complex ideas simple and easy to understand and repeat them often."

Taichi Ohno, explain things in an easy to understand manner

This is my simplified musings about life with a little bit of navel-gazing thrown in for good measure. I want to make a compelling argument so you say, "I can do that...I'm going to do that."

The reason why Toyota makes such a great car is that they are customer centered. Respecting their customers is at the core of their beliefs. This deep respect makes them serve their customer and produce a high-quality product that their customer will enjoy for decades. Most people buy Toyota and stick with that brand for a lifetime because they come to rely on the quality, reliability, and consistency of their cars. Toyota has clarity on their purpose and they have perfected the process to deliver it over and over.

In the same way, our relationships really involve two customers: the man and the woman. Two people that should be serving one another. We seek clarity and process because we respect ourselves and our partners. Without respect as the gravity that pulls us to gain clarity and develop a great process, we have nothing!

There are a few questions that we really need to ask to gain clarity, "What do our customers (aka our life partners) want?" I would say that most of us would say unequivocally, "I know," but we are absolutely clueless based on the state of most relationships. Divorce is at a record number and people are ready to kill each other in order to get revenge for the pain that has been inflicted. If we were doing it right, why are so many people unhappy? If we really knew what our partners wanted, why are we doing such a poor job of delivering it? There are really two sides to this question and this is the essence of the book. Not only do we not know what our partners want, but our partners are also unclear about what they want. If we did a better job of laying this out from the very beginning and getting total clarity, we wouldn't struggle to deliver the goods.

Total clarity and good process to stop the struggle

I interviewed Robert, who loves to sit and drink coffee and chat for hours, but his wife doesn't want to have anything to do with that. It's probably not a good match. It certainly would have been nice for him to know that before they got married. I imagine Robert has an empty spot in his life because that is something he loves to do and he can't enjoy doing it with the person he married. Inevitably, I would think he would look for somebody to fill that void.

Do the things you enjoy and find a partner that enjoys them with you

Another man I interviewed, Marshall, said he loves to joke around with sexual innuendos, but his wife doesn't want to have any part of it. One time he ran into his wife at the mall on his lunch break. When he saw her, he said, "Hey, do you think there's a dressing room around here that you can ravage me in?" Instead of his wife responding back, "Let's go see what we can find," her retort was "I'm too busy. I have to go grocery shopping."

You need to know the person you're with and you need to know yourself, otherwise, you're going to be frustrated and feel like something's always missing. Think about it, we designed superyachts, high-rise buildings, multi-million dollar houses, fantastic bridges, rockets, supercomputers, and phones that can just about do anything. All these are the result of careful planning and great designs, but how much time do we really put in the planning and designing our relationships that will last a lifetime? I can guarantee none of these amazing structures or designs are the result of somebody thinking this up in their head and never putting it down on paper. I am sure the detailed plans were drawn and revised many times.

Why wouldn't we give our relationships a little more due diligence? I will tell you what I think. First, people don't think it is natural to apply logic and process to their relationships. Secondly, I think we are afraid to bare our soul to ourselves, let alone let someone else know what we really think about some very important issues. Well, you know the old saying, "how's that working out for you?" Hey, I'm all about magnetism. I love the idea of love at first sight, but I am even more attracted to the idea of love for a lifetime. I think we need to take a serious look and make sure we deeply understand the person we're going to spend our life with. I'm convinced, more than ever, that most people are clueless about what makes them tick, let alone someone else.

So, if you're frustrated, your spouse is going to feel that frustration and more than likely, you will take it out on them.

In my first book *2 Second Lean*, it was the discovery that I was clueless about the way I was running my business that put me on the path to operational excellence. Prior to this discovery, I appeared to be a very successful businessman but, compared to the best companies in the world, I was clueless. For the love of God, I think it's time we all show a little bit more curiosity. So what's it going to be? A lifetime of marginal relationships or great relationships? Are you tired of stacking up more red blocks than green blocks? It was confronting the brutal facts that allowed me to turn my company around and build it into a world-class organization. So it is my conclusion that confronting the brutal facts about who we are and what we need is key. Taking an honest, deep dive into ourselves will allow us to experience fulfilling and meaningful relationships at the highest level. *(Go to the link at the end of the section to find 2 Second Lean.)*

Show a little curiosity and confront the brutal facts

Like anything in life, a great process that is clear and easy-to-understand will produce a favorable result. When it comes to relationships, I think clarity is a rarity and anything that resembles a process is considered heresy.

The One Thing
Great processes produce favorable results.

paulakers.net/ll-08

CHAPTER 9
Go and Watch

One of the most important concepts I learned about Lean is from Ritsuo Shingo. Ritsuo is the former president of Toyota China and the son of Shigeo Shingo, co-founder of the Toyota Production System. Ritsuo taught me if you really want to solve a problem, you must *go and watch*. You must gather the facts. Over the last 10 years, that is exactly what I've been doing. I've been watching and gathering the facts about the bad relationships men and women have, asking questions, and trying to figure out what is really going on. *(Go to the link at the end of the section to watch Total Participation video.)*

Here is one simple example of going and watching. I love the sun, I love the beach, and I love to surf. I am Greek and my skin was made to be in the sun. As a result, the beach became my laboratory where I learned and observed volumes about relationships. How many couples are holding hands and looking like they enjoy each other? The answer is very few. This is crazy when you really think about it. We're in the exact environment where people should be enjoying each other. We're not at work. There is no overbearing boss, no pressure… just sun, sand, surf, and ice cold beer. It is the optimum situation for couples to be happy and show it, but they're not! Most couples seem to be co-existing. They seldom look like they enjoy being together. Most people look like they're going through the motions, woe is me! When you see a couple that really enjoys each other, it's very different. They are holding hands, smiling, playing grab ass, touching and playing together in the water. They're communicating with their eyes and their bodies. I've seen this happiness with some couples but unfortunately, it's not that often. I would say it represents maybe 2 to 3 percent of people on the beach.

Another observation is there are so many people alone. They have nobody and that's even sadder. If you go on the basic assumption that there are about equal numbers of men and women, how come so many people are alone?

For many years I've been observing so many people alone and very few couples that look like they really love and enjoy each other. I always walk away from this observation thinking to myself, "Wow, so many people that have missed happiness.

How sad that everyone does not feel the joy of holding the hand of the one they love." I think that we were designed to love each other overtly for a lifetime.

Just like the production of a high-quality car that will last decades, I think the same thing applies to relationships. Is there a formula or clear process that stands a higher likelihood of producing a high-quality relationship that will last a lifetime? There are plenty of car manufacturers that are making average quality. For the first five years, things are good. Then everything starts breaking and it's time to sell it before the cost of maintenance becomes too expensive. Think about it! The analogy is so banging! Can you say trade-in, new model, an upgrade!

Lean is simply...the idea of doing things with maximum effectiveness. If you want to build a car, look at Toyota. They do it more effectively and with less defects than anyone else in the world.

If you want to live life with maximum effectiveness, apply Lean thinking to the way you live. Perhaps you might have a more desirable outcome. I know it looks risky to apply business principles to life, but I promise, you will be shocked at how awesome Lean is.

The Process in a Nutshell:
- Know yourself (write it down).
- Know the people you love.
- Review at least once a week.
- Evaluate your efforts and continuously improve them.
- Repeat for a lifetime and never be tempted to stop!

So this is the essence of a Lean Life. If you're not willing to write down who you are, what makes you happy and unhappy, and repeat the same process with the person you love, it will be difficult to have a lasting, loving relationship. It is difficult to please someone when you don't know what makes them tick. So, I'm begging you please, please, please stop what you're doing and begin writing. Every day, add a little bit more to the document. The next key is to read this document with regularity over the course of your lifetime.

This simple process will help you and the ones you love to build a lasting, loving relationship. Why? Because it removes the ambiguity of what you both want and need. It also gives you the ability to constantly be re-evaluating and adjusting so that you can be the ultimate partner. Could it be this simple? Most people think it's difficult to believe that Lean is as simple as fixing what bugs you and not about complicated technical jargon.

For my last example, I draw on something I learned in my book, *Lean Health*. 95% of your weight and health problem lies in what you eat. So if 80% of what you eat is fruits and vegetables, you will be in great shape. It's a mathematical truth and it's that simple. You gain weight in the kitchen and that is where you will lose it. *(Go to the link at the end of the section to find Lean Health.)*

What I'm saying is know yourself. Get to know the most important people in your life and know them well. Get to the root of the relationship. Do it with pen and paper and review this document with regularity for the rest of your life. It is this routine or Kata (the Japanese word for a regularly recurring habit) that will guarantee wild success.

The One Thing
Go and watch! Take careful inventory of what's really going on in your life.

paulakers.net/ll-09

CHAPTER 10
Let's Have Fun

I asked my good friend, Sven, "If there is one thing you want from a woman, what would it be?" Sven replied, "She has to learn how to have fun." He said, "When I was 19-years-old, I called up my girlfriend Karen. I asked if she wanted to go skiing at Big Bear for the weekend. She said sure, that sounds like fun. I picked her up and we drove up to the mountains, laughing and joking along the way. We checked into a funky hotel, not a five-star hotel, a very modest place, nothing special. We had a great time. When we woke up in the morning, we went skiing. While riding the chairlift, we were playful and we enjoyed every moment. It was amazing! We went to a cheap little restaurant, but no one complained about the food or that the service wasn't good. We went back to the hotel, fooled around, woke up in the morning, and nobody bitched at anybody. We just had a great time. Then we headed home. I dropped her off, kissed her goodbye, and said we need to do that again. There were no tension or mind games. It was just fun!

As life progresses, the next thing you know you're going to a restaurant or on vacation, and something is not good enough...the hotel is not good enough, the food is not good enough, the service is not good enough, or your attitude is not good enough. There's always a problem with something. Somehow or another we forget to have fun. Again, we only see problems instead of seeing how much we've all been given. We lose everything when we lose gratefulness."

Sven makes a fabulous point. He also says if his wife read this today she would ask "Who's Karen? Do you like Karen more than me?" Next thing you know, they would be in the bitch cycle of mind games instead of just saying let's go out and enjoy each other and have fun.

Weeks turn into years and your journey through life progresses. You've worked a long week and you wake up in the morning next to your wife. You roll over and start loving and kissing on her and then she says "Honey, can you change the lightbulb in the bathroom?" A long to-do list appears and the duty to maintain your stuff that makes up *the good life* smothers any chance of spontaneity. Sadly, the routines of living, slowly and quietly crowd out the fun, relationship building, and value-added time. It is replaced by non-value, relationship-killing time!

As a Lean thinker, I look at this situation and I ask myself what is the source of the problem? At first blush, I would say we all get caught up in the trappings of living: bigger houses, cars, and material possessions. We think somehow those things are going to satisfy us. The irony is, a lot of these possessions were obtained for fun, but they require an enormous amount of management, whether it be paying the bills, insurance, or maintenance. All these activities have the potential to interfere with being together and having fun. In the name of having it all, we inadvertently trade our fun time for things.

So what is the answer? We must identify what is true value-added activity in relationship building and not let anything stand in the way of those activities. We need to 3S (sweep, sort, & standardize) our life. We need to get rid of all the things that are stripping away and confusing us from the important work. Most relationships have a cluttered mess of crap. No wonder we don't get along. Just like a cluttered work area is unsafe and unproductive, so is a cluttered relationship.

I spend about nine weeks a year in Japan teaching and training people on the Toyota Production System. I often go to Costco to buy supplies and healthy snacks. I observed the most amazing thing with the Japanese people at Costco. For sure Costco is designed for buying in bulk...30 rolls of toilet paper and 12 rolls of paper towels, but the average family only needs one roll a week. In North America, we manage this dilemma by building bigger houses with more storage. The Japanese will have none of this. They love their minimalistic lifestyle and they will not let any North American influence change that. Their workaround is hysterical. They go in groups to Costco, buy everything they need, then split it up in the parking lot. The trip to Costco is not just a shopping experience, it's an event with friends and family. The communication flowing in their smiles is evident: they beat the system.

Fun requires spontaneity. You can't have spontaneity if you have a long list of life's burdens weighing you down. Spontaneity can create an element of surprise and I have never met a woman who doesn't love a good surprise. We all have so many responsibilities we can't even begin to think about being spontaneous, let alone surprising our lover with an emotional orgasm. With endless to-do lists, we might as well concede any chance of walking hand in hand on the beach and enjoying being present.

Value is in communicating to our partner that they're important and we do that by responding spontaneously to them in a playful and loving way. How in the world can we be playful and loving when we are caught up in the rat race of managing storage for 30 rolls of toilet paper and all the other stuff? Yes, all that extra inventory is just a giant detour that sucks our time and resources. Then we make it worse by piling on more stuff, increasing the burden on our relationships. It is total insanity and we don't even know it. The important thing is we must remember we are in control. We are the ones setting

Sorting groceries at Costco in Japan

up the processes that either support or detract from our relationships. They are not some mystical happening that requires a genie to understand. They do require us doing a few things:

1. ASK SOME TOUGH QUESTIONS
2. MAKE SOME IMPORTANT OBSERVATIONS

I will never forget my assistant Lori telling me "I love my new condo!" Lori and her husband Keith had just moved into a small condo from a large home. She exclaimed, "It was the best decision." I said, "Lori, how could this be? Your husband and you work from home. How can you do that from a 1,200 square-foot, two bedroom condo? You used to have a big house with a big yard and garden, and two dogs! How can you be so happy?" She replied, "Every weekend, Keith and I say to ourselves what are we going to do to have fun? We plan a hike, a drive, a new restaurant to try or town to explore. We don't have the burden to take care of a big house. There is no peeling paint to scrape or yard to mow. We can just enjoy each other and have fun."

Another friend of mine, Kevin Meyer, a great Lean thinker, told me about his house shopping experience. He and his wife were relocating and they were looking for a new house. The realtor kept pointing out all the great storage. Kevin replied back "We don't want more storage, we want less storage." The perplexed realtor couldn't understand Kevin's thinking. Everybody wants more storage! Kevin understood something that most people miss: things own you and the more things you have, the bigger slave you become. In order to have a Lean life, you have to fundamentally change your thinking. When you tour a Toyota plant there is just one banner hanging from the rafters and it reads "Good thinking, good products".

I told my friend Sven both these stories and he said, "You know, I remember when I was young and had nothing. We would drive down the road and would see big houses and say, 'wouldn't it be nice to have a big house like that?' That is the deception that we all fall for." Then Sven went on to say, "I had more fun when I was a young man driving around in a modest car with my girlfriend dreaming about the big house than I do now that I live in a big beautiful house." Folks, in the Lean world, the house is *inventory*. It represents *overproduction* and the rest is downhill from there. For me, it's all so simple when you understand where the value is and what's keeping you from having a meaningful fulfilling life.

Dreaming of that big beautiful home?

As long as we are not clear on where the value is in our life, we will always replace it with non-value added activity...wasted life, wasted emotion, wasted effort, wasted love, and most of all wasted time we could be enjoying with the people we love, smiling, laughing, building memories, and having lots of fun.

Spontaneity could easily be interpreted as *Just-In-Time*. Responsibility, in the form of houses, cars, and things, can easily be interpreted as *inventory*. It's all pretty simple when you start to see it like this. So what's it going to be? Do the math...less is more. It's not that things in and of themselves are bad, it is the excess that causes the problem.

One of my favorite quotes of all time is from Albert Einstein. Einstein, in all of his brilliance, explains the theory of relativity with a simple story, "If you touch a burning stove for a second, it feels like an hour. If you hold a beautiful woman's hand for an hour, it feels like a second." There's quite a few of us that have been touching hot stoves.

Albert Einstein

THE REAL DEAL

The One Thing
A garage full of toys is not the same as holding the hand of the one you love.

paulakers.net/ll-10

CHAPTER 11
Are You Happy?

Make no mistake about it, this is the most important chapter in the book. If you neglect to put down on paper who you are and what you need, this book will be a total waste of time.

Below is my document about who I am and what I have learned about myself. I have become this transparent for one reason: to help you. I want to set an example so you can see exactly what I did and how I arrived at my amazing life. In essence, what I've done was to document my process for life. Every day when I wake, I do it with thoughtfulness, clarity, and accuracy. I'm not making the same mistakes over and over again and producing defects, I'm doing life better!

As you read this document, know that it is now twelve years later, I have blown almost every goal completely out of the water. Here are is the list of my original goals:

- *Ran for U.S. Senate*
- *Traveled to 101 countries*
- *Flew around the world six times*
- *Was Interviewed by John Stossel*
- *Produced over 2,000 videos with millions of views on YouTube*
- *Created a radio show (now a podcast) called "The American Innovator"*
- *Crossed the North Atlantic three times in a single engine aircraft*
- *Completed 4 books, one of which was translated into 14 languages*
- *Was invited to the White House and had a conversation with George W. Bush*
- *Summited Mount Kilimanjaro and three other 14,000 foot mountains, and climbed to Everest base camp*
- *Honed my skills to become highly sought after, speaking in countries around the world to audiences of over 1,000*

For anybody that doubts the power of penciling out what's important to you, this document should be a clear testament to its value. I reviewed this plan once a week. I allowed Siri to read it back to me so it was deep in my brain and my psyche. I can't imagine the wasted life that would have occurred if I had not developed this simple process.

I let a few friends pre-read this chapter to get their feedback. One comment was they wanted to see my original list for comparison purposes. The list is not much different, just a continual refinement and adjustment as I gained greater clarity on the issues. The important thing is I reviewed the list every week, so I was constantly thinking about it and improving everything from the grammar to the content. Another comment was, "When I make this list, I'm afraid because it's going to force me to make a decision and I'm not comfortable with that decision at this moment in my life." Please don't be alarmed at this. When I made my list, I didn't stop everything I was doing and start down a new path. Instead, what I did was create clarity in the direction that I was heading and I started improving daily in all of these areas. As I reflect back, in one year I made so much progress! But it was not a sudden change. It was a gradual and consistent change.

The critical thing is that you start your list now! The moment you complete this chapter, write the first paragraph. In a few short pages, the answers you're looking for about life could be revealed. My thoughts about life are short, pithy, and brutally honest. This is my observation about my life at age 46, it all started with one simple question and I answered it with brutal honesty: "Are you Happy?"

It's too bad it took me this long to understand these simple, yet profound, concepts. My happiness or sense of wellbeing is directly linked to four things:

1. Being absolutely clear about my fundamental needs as a human being

2. Being absolutely clear about my biggest dreams

3. Having a crystal clear plan to meet my needs and achieve my dreams

4. Executing this plan by checking off daily habits and routines

Important note to the reader: I developed the Lean PD (Personal Development) App. Lean PD is a simple checklist that is phenomenal for developing habits that support doing life better. It is fast, easy to use, and intuitive. There are videos online that show you how it works. It is available on the iOS platform. *(Go to the link at the end of the section to find the Lean PD App.)*

I have discovered that in order for most of us to feel satisfied in life, we must feel like we are moving forward in life and continuously

Lean PD App

improving. The dreams we long for are not only possible but are drawing closer every day. These habits will directly support achieving these dreams.

The notion that someone might find happiness by mere luck is nonsense. It's achieved by a well-thought-out plan that is executed thoughtfully. I suppose it might be statistically possible that an individual could find happiness, but I prefer not to leave it to chance. In the same way, it's possible that someone could stumble into finding a great deal on a new car but I think you stand a much better chance if you have a plan and do research.

One of my favorite sayings from Samuel Goldwyn is, "The harder I work, the luckier I get!" It's not that I don't believe in destiny or fate, but destiny or fate have a much better opportunity to present themselves to someone who has properly prepared themselves. A half-hearted approach to finding fulfillment is a wasted life.

Why did it take me so long to figure this out? Because I felt there was no end to time. Many of us feel that way until we reach middle age. We then realize the clock is winding down and it's imperative that we don't squander time. A whole new generation will take our place and we will probably be forgotten. Hopefully, they will be smarter and better at using the time gifted to them. Perhaps if we get our act together and do something remarkable, the next generation will reflect back on the way we did it as a benchmark. They can even make the world that much better. It is the heightened awareness of time that brought me to the point of writing this document. Wake up, buddy! Time is not unlimited and life is not a rehearsal.

ARE YOU HAPPY?
The Goal

Being really happy is a lot more satisfying than being angry, frustrated, and generally unsettled about what exactly is going on every day. Lack of happiness seems directly related to a lack of clarity of goals and the necessary action steps to achieve them. At the same time, these steps are fleshed out, it is critical that other worthy opportunities do not hijack the happiness goal and ultimately derail the plan. This document is the equivalent to a well laid out process on the manufacturing floor. If you never had a process and you always relied on tribal knowledge, you can be sure there won't be clarity and consistency. I think the vast majority of people rely on having goals in their head, but it is the act of writing them down that brings the clarity necessary for wild success. It also gives you a reference point to measure your process.

The following document is the result of my close observation of successful people, who have traveled the world, treading paths few will follow. Documenting my life goals will create "deliberate practices" which will create tectonic change. At the same time, I will constantly "Hansei" and remold who I am, who I want to become and how I get there. I will relentlessly pursue the necessary steps to fully succeed in every area of life.

Important concepts that you must remember

WORDS: Your words are the most powerful and influential tool in the world. If you can clearly and effectively express ideas, you will have no limits. Master this and make it your strength.

PASSION: Bill Prymack, Doug Mockett, and my Dad had a passion for life that makes most people feel uncomfortable. Don't feel uncomfortable with your passion. Let it energize you to pursue your dreams. Many will misunderstand you. Press on and let your passion and desire to learn everything in life burn intensely.

WISDOM: Don't throw your pearls to swine (Matt 7:6). Your advice and wisdom is the result of the intense pursuit of continuous improvement and learning. Give your counsel freely to the curious and humble. The giving of your advice should be done judiciously. Do not disseminate your knowledge to those people who don't want to learn. This is the equivalent of shooting bullets without hitting the target, it's pointless. Choose with great care where you aim. It is critical you hit good targets!

Daily steps on life's wonderful journey

1. Exercise and build muscle for 5 minutes every day.

2. Answer all emails by 10 am. Answer all phone calls by 12 noon.

3. Make a list for all task management. Check 5 things off your task list by 5 pm.

4. Plan your day the night before.

5. Always remain positive and never give up

Life Defining Goals

Have a clear plan to significantly improve my life in the following areas:

1. Be highly respected intellectually by my peers.

2. Be extremely healthy.

3. Be continuously improving.

4. Have lots of fun.

5. Live by a checklist of daily habits.

6. Tolerate absolutely zero bullshit! Walk away the second someone pulls this. On second thought, run and never look back!

7. Create a clear mental vision of who I want to be.

8. Live to improve other peoples' lives. Change the world. Think crazy big thoughts. Teach Lean.

9. Be slow to speak. Two eyes one mouth.

10. Be curious and ask questions.

11. Be positive.

12. Treat mistakes as opportunities to learn.

13. Limit responses to 15 seconds. The 1-minute zone is no man's land. Nobody will be listening.

14. Increase my vocabulary by learning one word a week. Write and utilized those words. It's a powerful reflection tool.

15. Read one book a week. Take notes. Stop being a mental lightweight. Know history. It answers the why of the past and brings clarity for the future.

16. Listen to an audiobook every night before I go to bed.

17. Write one chapter a month for my newest book.

18. Never stop asking "Why" about everything.

Two Sides of Paul

Remember, inside of my mind there are 2 entirely different people:

FIT PAUL loves the adrenalin rush he gets from exercising daily. He skis without being winded. He has a clear image of a ripped body...like the cover of men's health magazine. He intensely pursues healthy food choices (2,200 calories a day): salads, fresh fish, and always a piece of fruit in his hand.

FAT PAUL is lazy and undisciplined. He eats without thinking about the long term consequence. He has no plan, no goal, and no satisfying results. He spends his life wondering why he's overweight and looks bad.

My Health Plan

Here is the plan I developed in writing *Lean Health*. This is one area I struggled with for years. In my original plan when I wrote *Lean Health* I wanted to weigh 185 pounds, down from 218 pounds, but I never got below 205 pounds. Then, in 9 months with *Lean Health*, I went from 218 pounds to 169 pounds. I am in the best shape of my life...the power of a thoughtful plan! If what you're doing is not working, take an honest look at it. *(Go to the link at the end of the section to find Lean Health.)*

The Plan

- *80% of my food is fruits and vegetables*
- *20% of my food is fish, chicken, and nuts*
- *No sugar or no artificial sweeteners*
- *No packaged food.*

- 2,200 calories a day
- *Log everything in MyFitnessPal App*
- *More than 10,000 steps a day*
- *100 push-ups and 200 sit-ups*

(Go to the link at the end of the section to watch My New Smoothie video.)

Life Action Plan

- *Delegate like a wild man (stop resisting because you think they are too busy...give it to them and watch them rise)*
- *Stay on top of projects*
- *Stay hyper-organized*
- *Have a perfect yard*
- *Have a clean shop*
- *Have an organized and well-maintained home and office (3S everything)*

Fun Action Plan

- *Ski four times in 2006-2007: Bachelor, Aspen, and Park City.*
- *Go back to Pittstown, New Jersey*
- *Attend Porsche racing school in 2007 and 2008: Porsche Masters*
- *Walk the Great Wall of China*
- *Attend concerts: James Taylor, Sugarland, Taylor Swift, Rascal Flatts, Carrie Underwood, and Sara Evans*
- *Fly to Bahía de Los Ángeles, dad's favorite place*
- *Hike in Aspen with Bill*
- *Take a glider class*
- *Learn to kitesurf*
- *Have lunch with Bob Taylor*
- *Play golf once a week with Leanne*
- *Learn 'Sweet Baby James,' 'Can't Help Falling in Love' and 'Up on the Roof'*
- *Buy a hot sports car and enjoy the hell out of it*
- *Spend a week touring Germany in a Porsche with Michael*
- *Climb Mt. Whitney and the Matterhorn*
- *Pilot a plane to Rome*
- *Pilot a plane around the world*

Zero Tolerances Action Plan
- *Have a great relationship with Leanne*
- *Stop denying myself of attaining what I want in life...don't put up with bullshit excuses.*
- *Embrace relentless improvements. It is a way of life and worth every effort. Dismiss anyone who doesn't understand this.*
- *Be excellent and you will attract people of excellence*
- *Welcome to constructive criticism. Listen carefully to the words people say because they can provide deep insights. Seek out people's opinions, but never let them put you down.*
- *Kick-Ass from here on out...NO EXCEPTIONS!*

Stop Doing Action Plan
- *Stop eating white bread*
- *Stop rationalizing why you can't lose weight*
- *Stop interrupting people*
- *Stop avoiding your email*
- *Stop buying anything unless it is the highest quality*
- *Stop using so much hyperbole*
- *Stop getting angry. It's an emotion that belittles you and does not help you achieve your goal of garnering respect.*

Start Doing Action Plan
- *Being tender with Leanne, Gods gift and the most beautiful flower to me*
- *Smile more and get everyone you meet to smile*
- *Bring out the best in everyone you meet*
- *Love every second of life...it's the seconds that add up to days of joy*

What I want my Dream Life to look like by December 2008
- *Easily maintain 185 pounds*
- *Own a state-of-the-art plane*
- *Maintain a spectacular garden*
- *FastCap LLC is in a new building and is getting recognition for it's deep commitment to growing people*

- *Be recognized and highly regarded for my intellect*
- *Be cutting edge and full of adventure*
- *Impact and inspire others*
- *Be creative. Be in an environment that facilitates explosive creativity.*
- *Make people smile!*

What my Teachers Taught Me

DAD
Stand out, lead, invest, learn, and be bold.

MOM
Love and encourage others. Be organized, clean, and devoted to family. Be tender.

LEANNE
Patience, discernment, and love of children.

BILL
Fly on my terms, take no chances, work long hours, know your product, and attention to details. Add a fourth axiom…know your competition, remember the little guy, and whatever you do don't get to the end of your life and regret anything.

WALLY
When an old man dies it's like burning down a library.

JON
Pause

PAMELA
Crystal clear vision.

JOEL
Pay attention to the bottom line, it affords you the opportunities you enjoy. Play the Devil's advocate. Protect the golden goose.

ART
Control my time. 'You get what you pay for.' Pay only what you want to pay, not what the other guy is asking. If you think someone is stealing from you, they are. Sell at the peak. If you spend $1,000

on your business, will you get a $1,000 back? Fly like a pro, hand on gear lever, and heads up on taxi.

JOHN
Nothing is foolproof, because fools are resourceful, so distance yourself from fools. Eyes are the best thunderstorm detectors, Trim up when low. Know your equipment and know your computer systems. They are stupid and do exactly what you tell them to do.

RUBEN
My wife is why I am successful. She is completely different and that different approach is a gift to any man who's smart enough to see it.

BOB CONRAD
Don't give away the farm and don't get distracted.

SVEN
Make sure you have a great sex life.

RON BELL
Take care of your health.

AUNT HELEN
Smile and be nice.

JEFF KAAS
Focus on your family.

JEFF GETZEN
Enjoy life. Hire horsepower. 1 out of 10 people are keepers...it's strictly a numbers game to find them.

DOUG MOCKETT
Live life to the fullest.

THOMAS EDISON
Opportunity is missed by most people because it is dressed in overalls and looks like work.

MIKE, NAVY SEAL
Every 30 days a significant opportunity passes in front of every human being...are you awake?

GARY PLAYER, GOLFER
The harder I work, the luckier I get!

DONALD TRUMP
Think big and kick ass!

COLIN POWELL
There are those who simplify and those who complicate. Those who simplify have real jobs. When asked how General Powell was going to defeat Saddam's Republican Guard he replied simply, 'We are going to cut them off and kill them.'

CHRIS MCCORMACK
You have got to have a mental strategy and a mental game. Question everything and ask the experts for their advice. Embrace the suck, when things get really tough and the pain is difficult, embrace it!

GEORGE H. BUSH
Nobody likes the big I am.

CHRISTINE
Never hurt a woman because they never recover.

JEFF BEZOS
Watch for hyper-growth, it can't be ignored. I learned something from everyone I meet.

ELON MUSK
Take it down to physics. Look for industries that are ripe for disruption. I have never seen someone endure so much pain, difficulty, and cataclysmic setbacks, and not give up.

BOB TAYLOR
Early money is better than late money.

Conclusion

Ten years ago, my life changed significantly because I took the time to write this document. It is essentially a life process document, equivalent to documenting a process and from that point on, improving upon it. The net result was significantly better. I felt better about myself, improved my overall sense of well-being, and lowered my frustration level.

I can't imagine what my life would look like today if I had not done this. What is really sobering is what my life would look like if I had done this at the age of 21. So much to learn and so little time...at least I didn't wait till my 60's or 70's to start this deep reflection process. I have interviewed so many people with regrets because they didn't have the basic tools that Lean has given. Those ongoing improvements dramatically changed my life. Instead of having an average life, it became remarkable.

This document has changed hundreds of times over the last ten years. I am constantly improving it, learning from it, reflecting on it, and adding to it. My hope is that by me being transparent and sharing with you my innermost thoughts, you too might be able to take a closer look and gather the facts about your life and your relationships.

YOUR WORDS
YOUR PASSION
YOUR WISDOM

The One Thing
Be transparent and discover what really makes you tick.

paulakers.net/ll-11

CHAPTER 12
Give Me Shelter

I will never forget when a friend said to me, "Paul I avoid home. My house is a mess, the garage is a mess, and the closets are a mess. It is all around chaos and there's not much to draw me there. Work, vacation, the mall, and my friends' houses are a lot more appealing, so I only go home when I need to." My takeaway was simple: your home should be a magnet, where you love to go...your refuge and shelter.

A mess...

The Rolling Stones wrote a famous song called "Gimme Shelter." I spent a good part of my childhood singing the famous chorus. Forgive me, but I'm speaking in the most general terms: men are hunters. We go out every day, see what we can conquer and bring home the spoils to our family. The last thing we want to hear from our spouse is, "You dumbass! Is that the biggest deer you can catch? We're going to starve if that's the best you can do. I saw the deer that Bob brought home to his wife, it was twice as big." Well, all these might be true statements but they are the most unsettling words a man can hear. If you add in a chaotic physical environment, you've got a recipe for a disaster. Men need their women to believe in them. When we come home we need shelter, not chaos or criticism. We need a place to regroup and clear our mind so we can get better and face the next day. If we are fighting the world and fighting at home doing life with a smile on your face becomes impossible.

Dale Carnegie said it best, "Don't criticize." This salient and powerful advice is timeless when it comes to our relationships. I have watched as husbands and wives tear each other down in front of friends and family. This is painful to watch as they wither right in front of us. While refraining from criticizing goes for both men and women, when women tear their men down, it is an epic folly. A man's ego is the size of a freight train and when his woman disrespects his effort's, dreams, and abilities, it is nothing short of castration, day after day. *(Go to the link at the end of the section to find Dale Carnegie's How to Win Friends and Influence People.)*

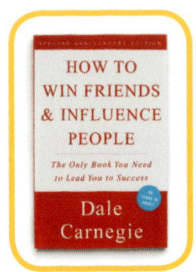

The same is true for a woman. Here's a story that illustrates the point perfectly. A woman on my Japan Study Mission, after learning that I was a pilot, stated she wanted to become a pilot and she looked into it but decided not to. When I asked her why she said her husband said it was nonsense! "Why would you want to do that?" he exclaimed. Her dream was burst. My reply to everyone is simple, allow your loved ones the space to explore their dreams. My response would've been, "Honey I think you would make a great pilot. Why don't you look into it and find out what's involved? I know that after you gather all the details you'll make a great decision." Whether

Support one another rather than tear each other apart

you're a man or a woman, a home should be a place where you can dream and work through issues together.

Taking care of the garden

At the end of the day, work is unique but home is a place where our family and our most important relationships reside...where you go for refuge. It needs to be viewed differently than just a place where you live. It allows protection so you can regroup and gain your mental and emotional strength.

I've always viewed my home as a place where I practice creativity and emotional expression. Whether I'm playing my guitar, writing a song, pruning a bonsai tree, building a piece of furniture or writing a book, my home is my refuge.

Some of you have seen my home. It is over the top, crazy beautiful, and the yards and architecture are a masterpiece. Most people say, "I can't imagine how much work it took to create 10 acres of artistic creation, let alone what it takes to maintain it." For me, my home is literally my artistic expression, where

Paul and Leanne's beautiful home

I can be a little boy and fearlessly play. I am constantly changing, improving, creating, exploring, and experimenting inside and out. My home is my art studio where I practice passion, patience, and creativity. *(Go to the link at the end of the section to watch My Home Woodshop video.)*

I made a profound observation after reading and visiting the homes of some of the greatest leaders in the world. From Thomas Jefferson's Monticello, George Washington's Mount Vernon, John D. Rockefeller's Kykuit, Winston Churchill's Chartwell, Dwight D. Eisenhower's farm at Gettysburg, Teddy Roosevelt's Sagamore Hill, Henry Ford's working farm outside Detroit, Eleanor Roosevelt's cabin alongside the Hudson River, Ronald Reagan's modest ranch in the hills of Los Angeles, or Donald Trump's Mar-a-Lago, everyone deeply expressed and lived their dreams in their refuge.

My home and refuge is the place where, after much soul searching, I created a better life, where I penned the document "Are You Happy?" It is the place where the world cannot get me and I have time to think. A place where I can practice continuous improvement, fail and learn.

Paul's office

A Lean life requires a place of refuge and creativity and the two are absolutely intertwined. You'll never experience true continuous improvement unless you have a safe place to express your thoughts and ideas. Develop that place, make it sacred, make it fun, but most importantly, understand its importance in the role it plays in your happiness. So, whether you're in a small apartment or a large farm, make it a refuge.

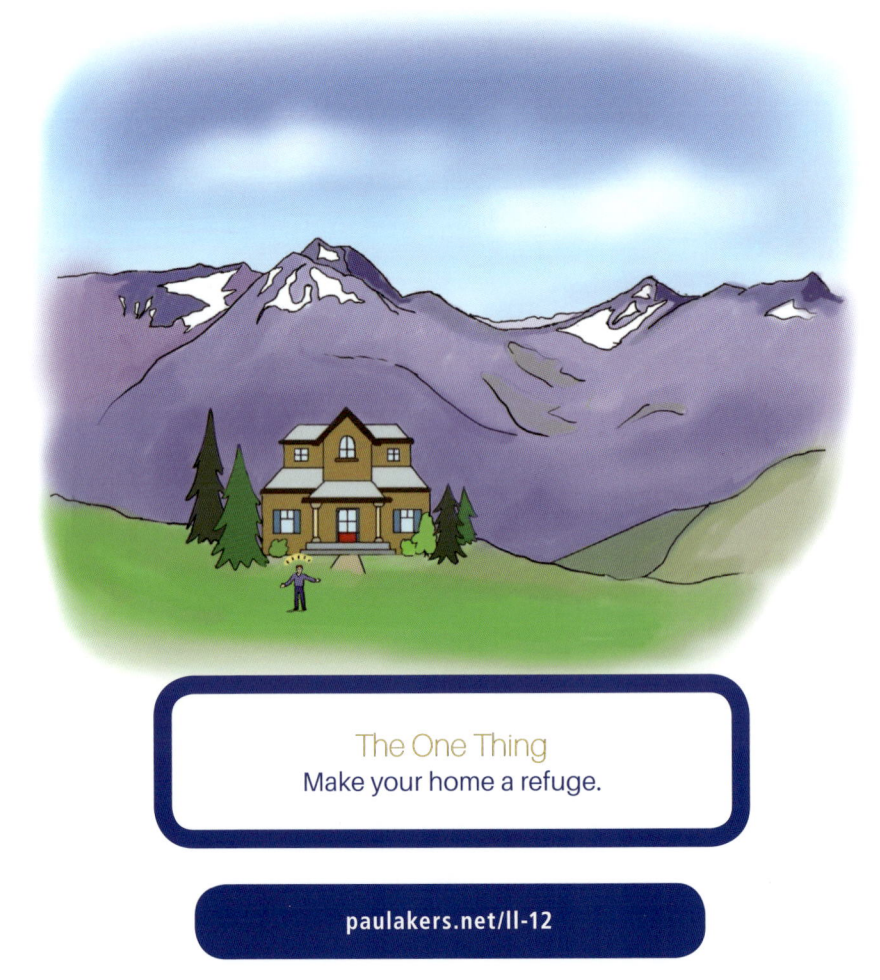

The One Thing
Make your home a refuge.

paulakers.net/ll-12

CHAPTER 13
Filling The Void

Let's face it, everyone wants to have a great life filled with great relationships and deep satisfaction. However, they may not be doing what it takes to have this experience. Think of how people fill their spare time binge-watching TV, playing video games, or on their phones. I would surmise they are trying to satisfy some missing element in their life. For the ones playing a game: action, excitement, or personal challenge. For the ones watching TV, perhaps it's some void in their relationship. Whatever it is, it wouldn't take much brainpower to figure out they are probably getting some form of substitution for the real thing. The idea of using this time for self-development or reflection is uncommon. Instead, most people are engrossed in mindless, short-term gratification rather than meaningful personal development. They are caught up in living a superficial, substitute life, rather than participating in a life of excitement, intrigue, and adventure. This is exactly the reality that I came to when I wrote: "Are You Happy?" I realized I was living vicariously through mindless gratifications. Then, in a flash or a satori (the Japanese word for awakening), I became disgusted with my substitute life and everything began to change.

I began developing my skills, abilities, and intellect, so I could personally experience everything that I subconsciously believed was only reserved for the select few. I saw with total clarity I could do anything if I was willing to apply deliberate and continuous improvement. I realized how much I had changed when my brother, who has an IQ significantly higher than mine, said to me, "Paul, you have become quite an intellect."

Paul, his mother, & brother

The most shocking thing to me is the phenomenon of filling the void is global. People in remote villages are glued to their phones instead of working or engaging with their friends and family. People are frittering away their time instead of developing their lives and relationships.

Dr. Victor Davis Hanson observed that when societies experience these extraordinary luxuries (such as cell phones, in the hands of 8-year-olds, that are more powerful than 10 IBM mainframes just a few decades ago), this time warp of reality, this luxury in any relationship can make you lazy… Luxury makes you lazy. "Hey, let me drop the supercomputer in your hands for just a few hundred bucks." When the same thing would've been a quarter of a million dollars just 20 years ago. Why go out and run, when you can experience it in 3D while sitting on the couch staring at your phone?

Mr. Amezawa says: "Money wrecks your brain." In the opening statement of my audiobook *2 Second Lean* I state, "Money suffocates creativity." *(Go to the link at the end of the section to find a link to 2 Second Lean.)*

> **Shigeo Shingo said there are four kinds of engineers:**
> 1. The white glove engineer
> 2. The Niet engineer (which is the Russian word for "No")
> 3. The catalog engineer
> 4. The engineer that washes his hands 10 times a day

Shigeo Shingo's reference to the catalog engineer is in line with the idea that, if we have abundance, we will choose to buy something, rather than use our creativity. We become lazy and miss the very essence of life: hard work, discovery, and resourcefulness. We have substituted them for a luxurious existence, devoid of hard work and diligence it takes to create this abundance. *(Go to the link at the end of the section to watch 4 Types of Engineer video.)*

While these statements are not absolutes, they have relevance and we should all be cautious not to let anything become a substitute for hard work, diligence, and personal self-development.

Dr. Hanson went on to say, in the presence of such incredible abundance, we somehow lose our collective sense of gratitude. The average person holds a phone that is more powerful than all the computers used to land a man on the moon. We have been born into a time that has afforded us so much! If we lose this collective gratitude, we will be separated from the true elements of life and create a substitute that will never satisfy us and atrophy our mind and spirit.

When I was in Bhutan, I was shocked that even in

Bhutan Market

this remote country people are affected by this phenomenon. As I walked through the outdoor markets, I noticed almost every vendor on their cell phone playing games.

It seems like we are all universally asleep. We no longer go for a run to experience an adrenaline rush. Instead, we mindlessly push buttons to receive a fake adrenaline rush not even close to the real thing.

When I spoke at Steelcase about *Lean Health*, I discussed how we have become a substitute society. We have substituted packaged food for real food, social media for real relationships, porn for meaningful sexual relationships, and video games for real exercise. *(Go to the link at the end of the section to find a link to Lean Health.)*

Steelcase

But of all the substitutions, I don't think any compare to our addiction to alcohol. Every evening, billions are bellying up to the bar to have a good time. Alcohol is the poorest substitution for a good time I think I've ever seen. Besides being incredibly expensive, it has no nutritional value and deep health ramifications. It screws up your most important asset...your brain. So many business professions are undermined by becoming fools with alcohol. Do I want to do business with a drunk? I don't think so! You don't have to look far to see the endless tragedies that alcohol has created. One of the most infamous examples is Teddy Kennedy and Chappaquiddick. I love Donald Trump's admonition to his children "Don't drink, don't smoke, and don't do drugs." It's that simple. He went on to say because he didn't drink, he had a strategic advantage over people who were constantly getting intoxicated. Don't get me wrong, I'm not a teetotaler. But alcohol has no hold on me...a glass of wine occasionally, but nothing more. Everything else is an abuse of my money, my body, my health, and my cognitive abilities.

I believe our substitute society is an attempt to fill a void in our lives with things that will never satisfy or bring true happiness.

When I was out of shape and overweight, I would eat for pleasure and because I was so stressed out. This was my way of filling the void that stress and anxiety had created. Food masked the pain but created more pain every morning when I look myself in the mirror. I have seen people spend thousands of dollars on clothes, shoes, and accessories to make themselves look better, when what they really need to do is stop eating the wrong food or too much food.

Recently, I saw a woman in a small shop in a third world country, with a $30,000 Birkin purse with clothes to match, thumbing through a stack of $100 bills, as she bought 30 more accessories. Some would say, "Wow, impressive." Not me. Maybe in my past life, but now I know better. I can afford to do the same thing, but I have no interest. I would have been impressed if she was fit or thoughtful, instead of rich and conspicuous. This is not intended to be an indictment on being wealthy and successful. But, I've learned the real sign of wealth are individuals with deeply engaged minds and physically fit bodies. That's impressive and it doesn't cost a dime. That's called *using your wits not your wallet*.

Have you ever noticed the people who are really fit don't need to wear a lot of clothes? Their statement is more about showing their fitness than the designer label. A fit body is the ultimate designer label.

I have seen people lethargic and uninterested while on the clock, but as soon as you get them on the basketball court or a baseball field they become crazy and competitive and play with intense energy. Why? We have become

Apply sports energy to your work

comfortable with finding substitutes for the things that don't satisfy. Why shouldn't our work and our jobs be extraordinary? It requires going to work every day and not thinking about doing the work, but how to do the work better. This simple but profound change in mindset can transform anyone's work into a game of continuous improvement, no different from competitive energy gained from participating in sports. It is that simple!

Essentially, we are distracted in exactly the same way an illusionist gets his audience to look somewhere else while the magic is happening. Stop looking in the wrong direction. What you're doing is looking at work instead of how to do work better. Work should be fun, engaging, enlightening, and gratifying.

Are you looking in the right direction

Don't fill the voids in your life with substitutes! Don't let it happen. It's a fake. It's a fraud. It's a substitute. The real thing is a thousand times more satisfying. This is one of the most important lessons I have learned about having a Lean life.

THE Real THING

The One Thing
Do you use fake, fraud, or phony substitutes?

paulakers.net/ll-13

CHAPTER 14
Paul's Conclusion

About a year ago, I began a new process on my Japan Study Missions. On the last slide of my presentation, I conclude the week's events. I found this process beneficial because it forced me to summarize the essence of our week. So here are the absolute non-negotiables and most important concepts of this book wrapped into six pithy bullet points.

1. **LIFE IS SHORT**
2. **LIFE SHOULD BE AMAZING**
3. **USE YOUR BRAIN**
4. **BRUTAL TRUTH EQUALS COURAGE**
5. **HIGH-QUALITY PEOPLE**
6. **FALL IN LOVE WITH LEAN**

Life is Short

Life is short and the meaning of this book will elude anyone who does not approach it from this critical vantage point. Life is not a rehearsal, it is for living right now. It is a gift that has been given to each of us. Life must be cherished and lived in a deliberate and thoughtful manner. A casual attitude is completely inappropriate for a gift of this magnitude. Start learning to say yes to all the amazing opportunities presented.

One of my favorite quotes from Thomas Edison is "Opportunity is missed by most people because it is dressed in overalls and looks like work!" Often these opportunities will not look sexy, exciting, or colorful. Let me give you an example: I was almost done with this book but I needed to find someone who understood where I was coming from to proofread the text. I wanted to be certain my points were clear and the examples supported my ideas. My good friend Filipe from Portugal, and fellow Lean maniac volunteered for this labor-intensive assignment. I will let him tell the story:

So there I was, watching my kids in their volleyball practice when I got an audio message from Paul: "Filipe, could you listen to my current draft of 'Lean Life' and provide some feedback?" To be honest, my first thought was, "I have a million things going on and this seems like a lot of work!" Nonetheless, I felt this intense desire to help Paul and make my contribution. Then all of a sudden, I didn't see it as work anymore, but as an opportunity to improve peoples' lives. The next thing you know, I'm burning the midnight oil making hundreds of revisions. Days turned into weeks as I worked with Paul to continuously make big and small improvements to 'Lean Life.' Not only did we improve the book, but we also improved the way we communicated and the entire editing process.

  Then the most amazing thing happened: I realized that I was actually helping myself...and helping myself a lot! As I reviewed the book, over and over again, I started to really understand the concepts at a deeper level. At 38 years old, with an amazing wife and two beautiful sons, we have all our lives ahead of us. What could be more timely than applying 'Lean Life' to bring more meaning to our lives? Every chapter is a playbook that will improve the life of my young family.

Instead of looking at this as "work" and asking "what's in it for me?" I viewed this as an opportunity to help others and it turned out to help me. "Every 30 days a significant opportunity passes in front of every human being. The question is...are you awake?" Look for ways to serve others and you will see those opportunities everywhere.
-Filipe

  I can't imagine what this book would look like if Filipe would not have dedicated so much time and energy to help improve it. Life has grand things in store for you. Wasting a single second hides opportunities that can transform you. *(Go to the link at the end of the section to watch Lean Portugal with Filipe & Tino video.)*

Life Should Be Remarkable

  Life should be remarkable, exciting, and forever improving in three critical areas: your work, your health, and your relationships. The notion of a naturally declining life is fallacious. I see people organize things they do around this defeatist attitude. Recently, when I was in Bhutan, I was hiking down from a Buddhist monastery with my guide Sangay. I said, "Sangay, what are the most important things in life?" His reply was fantastic.

  You must have Passion. Bhutanese people are passionate about their architecture and their natural environment. The flowing rice terraces define the landscape of this beautiful country. Whether rich or poor, every home is embellished. The architectural design of their monasteries is absolutely stunning. I jokingly quipped to Sangay that, "If you want to have the best lifestyle you need to be a monk, they live in some of the most beautiful settings in the world." Passion! You can see passion running throughout this society. The majority of their forests are old growth and untouched and they get the vast majority of their power from clean hydro. They refer to their water resources as white gold. All the animals run free. You can be driving down a road and right in the middle of the road there will be cows wandering with no supervision. There seems to be a true harmony to this approach. It exudes patience and calmness. While it is not normal for us Westerners, there is a beautiful element to so much harmony because of their passion for nature.

Then Sangay continued, "You must have Patience." Think about things a 1,000 times. Great things happen as you accumulate wisdom, patiently along life's journey.

The patience in which they have constructed the monasteries over hundreds of years and the way they go about their daily lives is remarkable. No one is in a hurry. You can often see road signs that say "No hurry, no worry." There is a clear rhythm of patience running through the Bhutanese people. *(Go to the link at the end of the section to watch Bhutan video.)*

Bhutan's beautiful elements of harmony

Lastly, Sangay said, "If you don't have health you undermine everything." One of my senseis in Japan, Mr. Takagi, who is 86 and his mother is 110 said, "The most important thing in life is health. From a beautiful body comes a beautiful spirit." Mr. Takagi recently just earned his Ph.D. and learned to speak fluent English. Remember, every element of life should be remarkable, settle for nothing but excellence and build a remarkable life!

Mr. Takagi From healthy body comes a beautiful spirit

Start Using Your Brain

Every life experience gives you the opportunity to gain wisdom. Wisdom is essentially a crystal ball that gives you the ability to look into the future and be a better predictor of outcomes. If nothing is changing or getting better, it's because you are not gaining wisdom from experiences. The reason you're not gaining wisdom is one of two reasons: You're lazy or you've chosen not to use your brain. When the wisdom warehouse is empty it will manifest itself at work, in your health, and in your relationships.

Crystal Ball

At work, it looks like, "I'm too old, the young people are too fast, they know technology too well, I can't keep up with it all. Even worse, the workforce is stacked against older people." What a bunch of crap and total nonsense. The power of applied wisdom and experience is much more potent than youth and all of its vigor. Anybody with half a brain understands this. But remember that you don't get extra credit for just showing up, you've got to add value to the organization. Whether you're younger or older, if your efforts are not remarkable or innovative, don't expect to be recognized, let alone elevated.

Regarding health, the most common excuses people tell themselves are, "my metabolism has slowed down," or "it's so hard," or "I travel all the time." All of these excuses are total nonsense.

Lastly, regarding relationships, "we just grew apart." The problem is you never took the time to know yourself and know your partner. Your processes, by which you engage and understand people, are the culprits. The best book to fully understand what I'm talking about is *How to Win Friends and Influence People* by Dale Carnegie. He spells it out in black-and-white, it is peoples' ability to relate to other people that make them happy. If you ignore this, it is at your own peril. Effectively relating to people is the most critical aspect of how you negotiate this life. You can do it with grace and thoughtfulness or you can do it on your own terms, which will more than likely reap a marginal result. Why not gain incredible wisdom from people who have made mistakes? My life would never be the same without the wisdom Dale Carnegie gained through his life experiences and recorded in his books, so we can dramatically improve our lives.

Brutal Truth Equals Courage

Remember everything of significance starts with a single action...courage. Bob Taylor, my mentor since I was 17-years-old, demonstrated this powerful principal when as a young man, he started Taylor Guitars. Bob says, "We believe at the heart of every great accomplishment you will find a single common ingredient: Courage. It's courage that allows us to explore. To push forward. To venture into the unknown. And while the decision to do so may seem obvious afterward, it wasn't at the time. Because each time we make the bold choice or go down the narrow road, we put something at risk.

Paul and Bob Taylor

Our ego. Our reputation. Our livelihood. Without courage we would never dare, we would change, we would never inspire..." Most people will not muster the courage to step definitively outside their comfort zone. As Bob says, "Every great accomplishment can be traced back to the seeds of courage." Do you have the courage to change your life? I can guarantee you, this is where the magic happens! You will never fill the voids in your life unless you have the courage to admit there's a problem and then take thoughtful and deliberate action. *(Go to the link at the end of the section to watch Bob Taylor "Courage" video.)*

High-Quality People

I see it over and over again, people do not have the courage to sort the bad people out of their lives. Bad people can usually be described as always propagating a sh*t storm around them and sucking the energy. They are negative and blame everything and everyone for their problems. They see the world through the filter of villains and victims, as opposed to personal responsibility. They are the antithesis of what this book is all about. Why is it that people will not sort bad people out of their lives? The usual excuses are, "they are really nice people," or "they have a lot of good qualities," or "they are a really old friend," or "they are my relative." If you're going to be honest with yourself, you just don't want to inflict any pain on yourself. Have the courage to surround yourself with high-quality people, who love to improve and take full responsibility for their position in life.

Next, get all takers and people who think, "What's in it for me?" out of your life. Remember, there are two kinds of people in the world: givers and takers. Your goal should be to become a world-class giver and surround yourself with other world-class givers. Get all takers the hell out of your life as fast and furiously as you can. I came to this realization early in life, when trying to negotiate the advantage or look for opportunities through the filter of, "What's in it for me?" As I matured and helped people without expecting anything in return I felt entirely different about myself. I began to attract and be attracted to other people who had a similar philosophy.

The next level of maturity was when I realized if I wanted to have a *Purpose*

Driven Life, to quote Rick Warren, I realized one thing, "It is not about you..." I observed that the people who believed this philosophy of helping their fellow man realized a depth of purpose in life that is not comparable to any other pursuit. There remains just one problem. For many people of this ilk, they are unwilling to separate the takers out of their life, and that undermines the full breath of their pursuit of helping others. It's without a doubt the most difficult part of this philosophy, but equally as important as becoming a world-class giver. *(Go to the link at the end of the section to find Rick Warren's Purpose Driven Life.)*

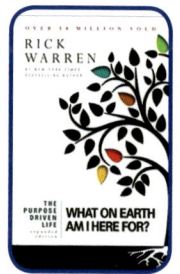

A direct application of this principle that I have developed is this, I am not interested in people liking me. I seek to win no popularity contest. There's nothing wrong with being a nice guy, but it's not the objective. What I do hope to achieve is to make a lasting and substantive effect on others. What I have learned is when people respect you, they will love you, and that's a much higher and significant pursuit and infinitely more satisfying.

Fall in Love with Lean

What I'm saying is falling in love with Lean will enrich your life. The daily pursuit of discovering solutions and learning from people will enrich your life beyond anything you ever imagined. *Bannish Sloppiness and Fall in Love with Precision.* Love the idea of being precise and getting it right. Live your life in a deliberate fashion so every process serves you. This intense desire to refine all of life's processes will energize you and deliver joy. Above all, do not relegate Lean thinking only to your business. It should be about the way you organize your life. This has been my prescription for my life and I am overjoyed with the fact that I have learned and applied these simple principles to my most precious gift: *life*! Now go live your life with meaning, passion, and intelligence and banish all excuses that are keeping you from achieving an extraordinary life! *(Go to the link at the end of the section to find The Key to Lean.)*

-Paul

Are you happy?

TELL THE TRUTH

> ### The One Thing
> Answer the question, "Are you happy?" Tell the truth and begin your *Lean Life* journey.

paulakers.net/ll-14